The Christian Life and Salvation

"It is supposed that we shall all be saved, that we are Christians from birth — and instead of the fearful effort of having to make use of this life for an eternal decision it is supposed that everything is already settled, and at most it is a question of whether out of gratitude we live a reasonably decent life, which in any case from the purely earthly and worldly point of view is the most prudent thing to do."

—SØREN KIERKEGAARD

The Christian Life and Salvation

DONALD G. BLOESCH

HELMERS & HOWARD

COLORADO SPRINGS

Published by Helmers & Howard, Publishers, Inc.
P.O. Box 7407, Colorado Springs, CO 80933 USA

Library of Congress Cataloging-in-Publication Data

Bloesch, Donald G., 1928-
    The Christian life and salvation / Donald G. Bloesch.
      p.   cm.
    Reprint. Originally published: Grand Rapids : W.B. Eerdmans, 1967.
    Includes bibliographical references and index.
    ISBN 0-939443-24-4
    1. Salvation.   2. Christian life—1960-   I. Title.
BT751.25.B5   1991
234—dc20

               91-16955
               CIP

Printed in the United States of America

To my wife,
my partner in pilgrimage

Acknowledgments

I wish to thank Dr. Philip Watson for reading and correcting this work. His suggestions have proved very helpful, although this is not to imply that his views are necessarily the same as mine. I am deeply grateful to Dr. John Mackay for his interest in this book and for writing the Foreword. I also want to express my thanks to Dr. Bela Vassady, the editor of *Theology and Life,* for granting me permission to restate parts of two chapters originally published in that magazine. Lastly I gratefully acknowledge my wife's painstaking reading of the manuscript in all its stages.

Foreword

The theme discussed in this small volume combines Christian centrality and contemporary relevancy.

At a time when the reality of a personal, dynamic, man-to-God relationship is not taken seriously in many Protestant circles; when terms such as "conversion," "piety," and "the inner life" are relegated to an outdated past; when it is even being rumored in theological coteries that "God is dead," this book, by a distinguished young theologian, takes on real significance. It is a vanguard symbol of a dawn that is breaking, of rediscoveries to be made, in the churches of historic Protestantism.

The issue of what salvation in its full Christian dimension means, crosses the boundaries of all church traditions and denominations. It is in the most vital sense an ecumenical question. It involves what God has done *for* man, and continues to do for man. It equally involves what God has done *in* man, and can do in man today, provided man is willing to respond to His loving gesture. This, it can be said, is the most crucial question that confronts Christianity and the ecumenical movement in our time. It is a question, moreover, inseparably related to the nature and mission of the church and to the meaning of the new humanity.

Evidence grows that concerned Roman Catholics in different parts of the world are posing the inquiry as to how Catholics can become "Christians." The same concern needs to mark the churches of historic Protestantism. What would be involved if

nominal Christians, whether Presbyterians, Lutherans, or Epis-
copalians, should give evidence that they had been gripped in
their personal thinking and living by the full dimension of salvation, by what it means to be "saved"?

The several chapters of this small book make an important
contribution to the central issue of contemporary Christianity,
that of giving present-day relevance to the meaning of Christian "sainthood," that is, to all that is involved in being "God's
men and women" in the mid-twentieth century.

The author provides luminous material for an intelligent
understanding of what God in Jesus Christ has done for man
and can do in man, and what man, through the Holy Spirit,
should do for God and for his fellow men. He shows that man
is truly man, and fulfills his human destiny when his life is God-
centered, and when his concern sweeps the full horizon of
human need in both church and society. Religion, he points
out, may not become a purely private or churchly matter. Faith
is not merely passive acceptance by men of what God has said.
It is the passionate devotion to God the Giver and to His will.
The Kingdom of God, it is well said, is not merely a gift; it is
also a task. Men cannot have the truth in the full Christian
sense unless the truth has them, so that they *do* the truth. For
Christian truth is a Person, and to be truly Christian means to
be "saved" by Him who becomes one's Lord, and whose lordship extends over the soul and the church, over society and
the state.

This book will help its readers to realize that in a Christian
context "saving" truth is more than a bird to be pursued, or a
badge to be worn; it is a belt that braces one for action on the
road of life.

                                                    —JOHN A. MACKAY

Table of Contents

Introduction

In this ecumenical era there is a need to re-examine the role of the Christian life in our salvation. Whereas Catholic and evangelical theologians agree that the Christian life is the response of the Christian to the salvation won for us by Christ, they tend to differ on how such a life is related to the appropriation and fulfillment of this salvation. The Reformation concern has been to preserve the divine initiative in the whole process of salvation; the Catholic concern has been the pursuit of holiness. Whereas the Reformers held that glory belongs to God alone (*soli Deo gloria*) and that salvation is only by His grace, Catholic theologians have emphasized the need for a holy life. In Reformation theology the justification of God is the guiding motif; in Catholic thought the accent is placed on the transformation and sanctification of man.

It must be recognized that there is no absolute dichotomy between these two types of Christianity, for each makes a place for divine grace as well as personal holiness. Yet in Catholic and Protestant dogmatics these two concerns have not been given the same emphasis. We shall attempt to do justice to both the ideal of perfect love and the message of free grace. The call to holiness which has been preserved (although not always in its biblical context) in Catholic piety (both Roman and Orthodox) and also in the circles of sectarian revivalism must be held in tension with the biblical and Reformation witness that salvation is by grace alone (*sola gratia*) and faith alone (*sola fide*).

The chief problem that we shall deal with is how the re-

13

sponse of the Christian is related to the realization of his salvation. In answering this question it is incumbent upon us to avoid two errors. One of these is the separation of the Christian life from salvation. The other is to make the Christian life the foundation or ground of our salvation.

To separate the life of the Christian from the salvation of God is to divorce ethics from religion. It was precisely this non-ethical religion or religiosity that was attacked by the Old Testament prophets and by many saints and reformers through the ages. Such religion may take the form of either ceremonialism or antinomianism. The biblical prophets did not call for ritual sacrifices but for the sacrifices of obedient lives. Jesus, too, placed the emphasis on inward loving obedience rather than on outward or merely formal acts of piety. Modern culture religion has certainly separated the gospel from the concerns and practices of daily life, particularly life in its social dimensions. When religion becomes a private or churchly matter then it has lost its prophetic and regenerating power.

The other basic error is to make the Christian life the foundation or cornerstone of salvation. In this case we have a religion of ethical culture. Our salvation is then dependent on our works. Right conduct becomes more important than divine grace. One is now in the pitfalls of moralism and legalism, which assert that our salvation can be won by a moral life or by obedience to the law. Such works-righteousness is to be found not only in humanistic liberalism but also in much of conservative Protestantism, despite its outward adherence to the message of free grace. When our salvation is made contingent upon our acceptance of particular confessions of faith or the way in which we interpret Holy Scripture, then we are once more in the sphere of legalism. The post-liberal "secular theology" (van Buren, Wm. Hamilton, Cox, J. A. T. Robinson) tends to make salvation equivalent to neighbor-love and humanization and thereby severs Christian life from its religious and transcendent basis.[1]

Roman Catholicism has sought to guard against the preceding

---

[1] See explanatory note 1. All explanatory notes are found on pages 141-153.

errors by upholding divine initiative in salvation and yet making a place for meritorious works on the part of the Christian.
Salvation is by grace, but good works are the condition for the
increase of this grace. In Roman Catholic scholastic theology
man cooperates in his justification on the basis of prevenient
grace. He can merit salvation and even make satisfaction for
sins but only with the assistance of grace. One can appreciate
the emphasis on human responsibility in Catholic theology and
the upholding of the ideal of Christian perfection. Yet Catholic
thought tends to fall into a kind of synergism by which we are
saved by grace *and* works. Catholic theologians stress the paral-
lelism of divine and human action, but what is needed is an
affirmation of the paradoxical unity of this action.[2] It must
be acknowledged that the paradox of salvation in the biblical
sense has been grasped by many who stand in the Catholic
tradition and that in this ecumenical age new attempts are
being made by Roman Catholics to restate this whole problem
in a fresh way.

Reformation theology and modern neo-orthodoxy (Barth,
Brunner, Reinhold Niebuhr) have endeavored to bring together
divine grace and the works of faith and love by viewing the
latter as an effect or fruit of the former. The Christian life is
consequently only a sign of our salvation; the effecting of salvation is regarded as the work of Christ alone (*solus Christus*).
Karl Barth in particular has stressed the sole efficacy of the
atoning sacrifice of Christ in our salvation. Brunner and Niebuhr have remained closer to the Reformers in seeking to include the decision of faith in the event of salvation. Yet the
Christian life understood as works of love and obedience is regarded by these men also as a sign and by-product rather than
a means of salvation.

Our position is in line with the main thrust of the Protestant
Reformation. The sole foundation of the Christian life must
be regarded as the justification of the ungodly (*justificatio
impii*). The free grace of God is the basis of our salvation, and
faith is the necessary response. At the same time we seek to
move beyond the Reformation by giving a more positive ap-

2 See explanatory note 2.

praisal to the Christian life in the working out of our salvation. The Reformers talked much of a "holy gospel" and a "holy faith" but very little of holy persons. They sounded the call to repentance, but they neglected the call to perfection. Their emphasis was on the sinfulness and helplessness of man apart from God, not on man's ascent towards sainthood made possible by the Holy Spirit. This is not to deny that both Calvin and Luther had a doctrine of sanctification and that both theologians sought to make a place for works of love in the drama of redemption. At the same time the tragic circumstances and conflicts of their time prevented them from developing a doctrine of evangelical perfection and relating this in a meaningful way to the fulfillment of Christian salvation. The Reformers were correct that we are justified while we are yet in our sins, but they did not give adequate recognition to the fact that we are not glorified until we have been made holy. They were zealous to uphold the sovereignty of a gracious God, but they did not give sufficient attention to the interior life of devotion and the need for ascetic disciplines (although such disciplines were never lacking in their own lives). The devotional life was generally ignored in post-Reformation orthodoxy, and it has yet to be given its rightful place by the neo-Reformation school of theology.

It remained for the Pietists and the Puritans as well as the Evangelicals associated with the eighteenth-century awakenings to give the proper attention to the cultivation of the spiritual life.[3] These movements represent the fulfillment of one side of the Reformation in that they sharpened and developed ideas that had already been expressed by the Reformers. At the same time they tended to neglect the sacramental and ecclesiastical emphasis of the Reformation, particularly in their later phases. They also gave minimal attention to the doctrine of creation which accounts for the otherworldly orientation of much of left-wing evangelical Protestantism.

Our position is that the Christian life is the arena or theater of our redemption and not simply an effect or sign of this redemption. It is the battleground on which our salvation is con-

[3] See explanatory note 3.

tinually fought for and recovered. The Christian cannot earn his salvation, but he is called to retain and defend it. The Christian life is not the basis or source of our salvation, but it is an integral element in our salvation. It is a necessary fruit of our justification and a means to our final salvation. We are saved *by* grace alone, but we are saved *for* works and also *through* works in the sense that works that proceed from faith serve the advancement of our sanctification.

Our good works are not the cause of the increase of grace, but neither are they simply a by-product of grace. They signify not an appendage to our salvation but the flowering and fruition of our salvation. With the Reformers we hold that faith is not deficient concerning our justification. Faith does not need to be perfected by love in order to justify us. But faith seeks and points to the sanctification of man. The basis of faith is God's justification; the intention of faith is man's sanctification. The Christian life is the working out of faith to its fulfillment.

The church has always been beset by the heresies of objectivism and subjectivism. We are in the morass of objectivism when we center salvation in a finished secret decree of God, or in the cross of Christ as past history, or in the sacraments. The peril of subjectivism is present when salvation is centered in private mystical experiences, value judgments, a crisis of conversion or the inner light.

We need to break through the object-subject antithesis (Brunner). We must affirm both God's decision for us and our decision in God. We must try to grasp the paradoxical unity of what God has done for us in Christ and what we can do in, with, and for Christ. Moreover, our decision for Christ must be seen as more than simply one crucial experience; it must be regarded as none other than the Christian life. Faith signifies not only passive receiving but also wholehearted and life-long devotion to Jesus Christ.

In line with the testimony of both Catholic and evangelical traditions we affirm that the Christian witness must be one of deed as well as word. Our witness must include not only the proclamation of the Word but also the demonstration of a Christian life. It should entail not only an expounding of the

Scriptures but an identification with the travails and agonies of our fellow men. We are truly serving Christ when we seek to serve the outcasts and underdogs of society.

A life of faithful obedience must be viewed as having an organic relation to our salvation. It is a necessary fruit of the salvation wrought in the past on the cross of Calvary and also a divinely ordained means by which this salvation is realized in the present. It also witnesses to and prepares the way for the fulfillment of salvation in the future. Justification is made available to the ungodly, but only those who seek to live a godly life reap the full benefits of this justification.

The way to salvation is Jesus Christ. But we here have in mind not only Christ *for us,* but also Christ *with us* and Christ *in us.* This means that the way to salvation entails not only Christian belief but also Christian life. Christian life is life that is grounded in the cross of Christ and empowered by the Spirit of Christ. It is life that shares in the love and outreach of Christ to all peoples. Life in Christ is life that is separated from the world in its sin and selfishness and consecrated unto God. Yet it is also an involved life, one that is in solidarity with the world in its suffering and anguish. Christian life is a sign and mirror of the death and resurrection of Jesus Christ. It is also a pledge of His coming triumph at the end of time, when the kingdom of this world shall be transmuted into the kingdom of God.

I

The Plan of Salvation

Perhaps the most elemental question that man has ever been moved to ask is the soteriological question — "How can I be saved?" This question cannot be properly formulated, however, until one has a true understanding of the misery and predicament of man. But man on the basis of his own resources is unable to perceive the nature of his disorder. The crux of this disorder can be known only in the light of God's redemptive acts mirrored in the history of the Bible and culminating in the cross on Calvary. Indeed, it is not until we are confronted with the love of God manifested on Calvary that we can appreciate the heinousness of our sin and the depth of our misery. We also cannot know the nature of the salvation that God desires to give us until the encounter with Jesus Christ. The soteriological question presupposes an inner knowledge of a plan of redemption that has its pivotal center in Calvary but will not be consummated until the end of the world. It is not until God's will and purpose for mankind have been unveiled to us that we can discuss intelligibly either the plight of man or the hope of man.

The plan of salvation is presented in Holy Scripture, but in such a way that it is not immediately accessible to human understanding. We can gain some intimation of this plan through faith, as it is stated in Ephesians 1:9, 10: "For he has made known to us in all wisdom and insight the mystery of his will, according to his purpose which he set forth in Christ as a plan for the fulness of time, to unite all things in him, things

19

in heaven and things on earth." God's purposes appear to be
mysterious, but they can be known partially through the Spirit
of God (cf. Eph. 3:3-5). To the senses God's ways are "in-
scrutable" and "unsearchable" (Rom. 11:33). But with the
eyes of faith one can discern meaning and purpose in God's action in the history of the Bible and also in world history. A
design of salvation can be recognized by those who have eyes
to see and ears to hear.

Yet even for the man of faith, the divine plan of salvation,
because of its magnitude and intricacy, still appears to be
shrouded in mystery. The believer can express this mystery
only in terms of symbolism and paradox. "Paradox" in this
context signifies a category by which one can discern the significance of eternal truth. Kierkegaard defined a paradox as
"an ontological definition which expresses the relation between
an existing cognitive spirit and eternal truth."[1] The paradox
invariably takes the form of a contradictory statement. Yet the
contradiction is due to the limitations of our reason. In God's
sight there is no contradiction. The offense of the paradox is
due to the pretensions of our reason.

The category of paradox is admittedly philosophical in ori-
gin, but a philosophical category can be made to serve the Word
of God. This category is certainly not foreign to the inner
meaning of the Bible, since paradoxical statements abound in
the Bible. It can be said that this category definitely lends itself
to theological appropriation. Stendahl maintains that strictly
logical thinking is alien to the world of the Bible. He has written: "Over against stringent logic stands Jewish thinking in
images, where contradictory facts and conceptions can be put
together in a kind of significant mosaic."[2]

Kierkegaard, who helped theology recapture the meaning of
paradox, contended that there is only one absolute paradox.
This is the paradox of God in man and man in God in Jesus
Christ. In theological circles this is known as the Christologi-

[1] Søren Kierkegaard, *The Journals of Søren Kierkegaard*, ed. and trans.
Alexander Dru (London: Oxford University Press, 1951), p. 194.
[2] Anton Fridrichsen, *et al.*, *The Root of the Vine* (New York: Philosophical Library, 1953), p. 67.

cal paradox. But this paradox can also be regarded as a soteriological paradox. It signifies both the divine election of
Jesus Christ and His obedient decision. Christ is not only our
Saviour but also our Pattern, and therefore the fulfillment of
our vocation can be said to be analogous to the realization of
His vocation. This means that the salvation we receive as well
as the salvation He accomplished can be expressed only in paradoxical language.

Unfortunately, most theological systems are not oriented about
the paradoxes of Christ and salvation. Although the facets of
salvation are interrelated, theologians have tended to separate
them or arrange them in logical sequence. This has been true
particularly since the Enlightenment. We can see here the
influence of Descartes, who maintained that clarity is the norm
for truth. Descartes held that an idea is not valid unless it is
clear and concise. But it must be recognized that natural reason
in every age craves a logical, air-tight system. It is the very
nature of reason to shrink from mystery.

The concept of the order of salvation (*ordo salutis*) connotes
an attempt to explain the paradox. This concept played an
important role in Reformed and Lutheran orthodoxy. The
theologians of orthodoxy were right in maintaining that there
is a sequence in our salvation. But they did not fully discern
the fact that each facet of salvation participates (at least to
some degree) in every stage of this sequence.

There have been various interpretations of the *ordo salutis* in
the history of the church. Paul himself alluded to an order or
plan of salvation; yet he was careful to safeguard the paradox
that salvation is entirely of grace but man is at the same time
fully responsible for decision and obedience. As has already
been indicated, Paul refers to this evangelic plan as a "mystery."
In his mind the broad outline of the plan can be known, but
how God actually accomplishes this plan in history without
overriding man's freedom eludes rational comprehension.

Paul enumerates the different facets of salvation in Romans
8:28-30. First there is foreknowledge, then predestination, then
calling, then justification, and finally glorification. Some theologians have placed the atonement after predestination and

sanctification after justification. What many overlook is that in
verse 28 Paul avers that God calls those who love Him, thus
not closing the door to human responsibility. Verse 29 centers
about Jesus Christ, indicating that our predestination has no
meaning apart from our conformity to the image of His Son.

In II Thessalonians 2:13-15 Paul again refers to an order of
salvation. But this order is neither strictly logical nor chronological. In these verses predestination is organically related to
sanctification and faith. Glorification is pictured as an attainment as well as a gift. In verse 15 there appears to be a warning
that predestination will be forfeited unless we "stand firm" in
the faith.

The paradoxical relationship between the various facets of
salvation is found not only in Paul but throughout the Bible.
In Psalm 84:11 we read that it is God who bestows grace and
honor, but only those who walk uprightly receive His gifts.
Isaiah speaks of God's plan as being inexorable and final (Is.
14:24; 25:1), but at the same time he makes salvation contingent on the contrition and obedience of God's children
(30:15, 18). The book of Jeremiah tells how God elected and
consecrated the prophet before his birth (Jer. 1:5); yet Jeremiah is depicted throughout the book as free to turn away from
God and resist Him. The Synoptic Gospels speak of only a few
being "chosen" (cf. Mt. 22:14; Mk. 13:20; Lk. 10:21, 22), but
at the same time they issue a universal call to repentance. In
the Fourth Gospel, immediately after Jesus reveals that "the Son
gives life to whom he will," He makes eternal life dependent
upon hearing and believing His word (Jn. 5:21-24). The book
of Acts, which calls the church to the missionary task, at one
place appears to make faith rest upon predestination (Acts
13:48).

The church through the ages has sought to overcome the
seeming contradictions and ambiguities in Holy Scripture concerning the plan of salvation. But for the most part the theologians of the church have either blunted the impact of God's
foreordination and election in order to do justice to personal
decision and faith, or else they have closed their eyes to the
necessity for faith and decision in the interests of a high doc-

trine of predestination. In the mind of the Bible, the kingdom is not only a gift but also a task. The doctrine of salvation is compromised unless both of these realities are held together in creative tension.

The Council of Trent in the sixteenth century attempted to state the Roman Catholic position on the order of salvation.[3] Aristotelian categories were utilized with some modification in an effort to make this order intelligible. The final cause of our salvation is spoken of as the glory of God and Jesus Christ. The efficient cause is the merciful God who washes and sanctifies and anoints us with His Spirit. The meritorious cause is Jesus Christ. The instrumental cause is the sacrament of Holy Baptism. The formal cause is the justice of God whereby He makes us just through the Holy Spirit. Although it is true that the relationship between these causes is very complex and that each cause is present on every level, it is questionable whether this kind of explanation adequately safeguards the mystery in the divine plan.

Calvin and Luther were more true to the paradoxical nature of the plan of salvation, but they also sought to rationalize this plan. Luther displays an acute awareness of the paradox of salvation in his *Commentary on Romans* (1515), but in his *The Bondage of the Will* (1525) he appears to have lost sight of this paradox, and he reduces man to little more than an automaton. The influence of Aristotle's philosophy can be seen in Calvin's attempt to explain the sequence of salvation in Book II of his *Institutes*.[4] Calvin states that the efficient cause of our salvation is the love of God the Father; the material cause is the obedience of the Son; the formal cause is the illumination of the Spirit or faith; the final cause is the glory of God's great generosity. Here one can discern the bent towards objectivism in Calvin's theology.

Benjamin Warfield, who represents the infralapsarian view-

[3] The Canons and Decrees of the Council of Trent, Sixth Session, Ch. VII. In Philip Schaff, ed., *The Creeds of Christendom* (New York: Harper & Bros., 1919), II, pp. 94, 95.

[4] John Calvin, *Institutes of the Christian Religion*, ed. John McNeill, trans. Ford Lewis Battles (Philadelphia: Westminster Press, 1960), III, 14, 21, p. 787.

point in Calvinist orthodoxy, also sought to explain the order of salvation in objectivistic terms.[5] Warfield states his position in his book *The Plan of Salvation*. First, he says, there is the divine permission for the fall; then follows the election of some to life in Christ. After this is the gift of Christ for the redemption of the elect. Then there is the gift of the Holy Spirit to save the redeemed. Finally we have the sanctification of the redeemed.

A slightly different approach to the problem is to be found in the Westminster Confession. This confession, adopted in the seventeenth century, makes justification, adoption, and sanctification dependent on effectual calling through the ministry of the Word. Predestination and the atonement precede effectual calling. The relation of the eternal decree and justification is spelled out in Chapter XI, Section Four of the Confession: "God did, from all eternity, decree to justify all the elect and Christ did, in the fullness of time, die for their sins, and rise again for their justification; nevertheless, they are not justified until the Holy Spirit doth, in due time, actually apply Christ unto them." Despite the fact that the confession opens the door to ecclesiasticism, it has the merit of trying to take seriously the subjective dimension of our salvation.

Karl Barth has subjected the soteriology of the Reformation to a radical reappraisal. He has rightly seen that salvation must be grounded in Christ rather than in a secret decree in the mind of God. According to Barth the election, justification, and sanctification of all men took place in the life and death of Jesus Christ. The *ordo salutis* is not a series of different acts of salvation but rather different aspects of the one great act of salvation accomplished in Christ. The goal of salvation is said to be glorification. It is well to note that Barth retains and even gives heightened significance to the conception of extrinsic justification, which means that justification takes place completely outside ourselves (*extra nos*).

[5] Infralapsarianism views the decree of redemption as following the fall of man, whereas supralapsarianism holds that this decree precedes the fall, which itself is predestined. Calvin and Barth are both to be placed in the supralapsarian camp.

This is not to imply that Barth does not make place for the subjective apprehension of our justification and reconciliation. It is his view that this salvation must be acknowledged and apprehended in faith. Yet he maintains that faith is subsequent to rather than concomitant with justification. "It [faith] is not the event of the redemptive act of God. It can only follow this. It is subsequent and at the deepest possible level subordinate to it."[6] For Barth faith is not included in the event of redemption but rather is an awakening to the redemption already accomplished in Jesus Christ. It is questionable whether he does justice to the biblical truth that the objective occurrence and the subjective apprehension are two sides of the one event of justification (or redemption), and that neither has effect apart from the other.

We suggest an order of salvation that mirrors the dynamic and paradoxical character of the biblical proclamation. Because there is an infinite qualitative difference between God and man (Kierkegaard), there are really two perspectives of the order of salvation, a human and a divine. It can be shown that these two perspectives or two orders are held together in paradoxical relation throughout the Bible. From the human or temporal side, our salvation begins in seeking for the help of God. The next step is repentance and faith. This second step might more accurately be termed "surrender, repentance, and faith," inasmuch as an initial surrender to God's Spirit (which is in reality the first phase of faith) takes place prior to repentance and a steadfast trust in God. We could not repent and make a full surrender to Christ unless we were overwhelmed by the love of God and convicted of our sin. The third step is obedience in faith culminating in the final step — perfect love. This last stage might also be termed "perfection in love," since the love of God so permeates man's entire being that man loves perfectly just as God loves. The eternal order is slightly different. First we have predestination, then justification, then sanctification, and finally glorification. Our contention is that a

6 See explanatory note 4.

man who is wholly perfected in love is at the same time in a
state of glory. The two perspectives are pictured below:

Temporal Order	Eternal Order
seeking for help	predestination
repentance and faith	justification
obedience in faith	sanctification
perfect love	glorification

This picture of salvation must be recognized as being only a
picture and not a purely chronological schema. There is a
chronology in both God's acts and man's responses, but God's
time and man's time are not on the same level. Because of the
qualitative difference between the two types of time (or between
time and "eternity"), the beginning of the plan of salvation is
not to be located simply in the past, nor the consummation
simply in the future. Rather, both the source and completion
of the plan are to be located in God. Therefore, in order to
know the full dimensions of the mystery of our salvation we
must look not only backward and forward into history but also
upward into heaven. It is only when the kingdoms of this world
are transmuted into the kingdom of God that these two orders
shall become one; then we shall know even as we are known
(I Cor. 13:12).

Some further observations must be made about this picture.
First of all, the two orders do not signify two parallel or independent processes, but rather two ways of describing the working out of man's salvation to its fulfillment. Again, it should be
recognized that each facet of salvation is correlative with the one
opposite. For example, seeking for help is correlative with predestination, and repentance and faith are integrally related to
justification. Also it must be noted that the prior terms, in that
they are realized and consummated in the others, are included in
the subsequent ones. Seeking for help is included in repentance,
obedience, and even perfect love. Predestination is included and
realized in justification, sanctification, and glorification. Certainly the prior facets of salvation also include the subsequent ones
by anticipation. The perfect love of Christ is undoubtedly ex-

perienced in a fragmentary way even by the man who begins
to seek the help of God, but perfect love as a permanent state
is enjoyed only by the glorified saints.

We must also affirm that none of the categories in this schema
has any meaning apart from Christ. We are predestined, justified, and sanctified in Christ. We can only believe and obey
when we are centered in Christ. But God the Father and the
Holy Spirit also play a role in our salvation. Our salvation takes
place in Christ, but the sacrifice of Christ is made possible by
the compassion of the Father, and it is made efficacious by the
action of the Holy Spirit. Our salvation is *in* the Son, but it is
from the Father and *through* the Holy Spirit.

We have attempted to enumerate certain dominant categories,
but there are other facets of our salvation that might be included. Among these are adoption, mystical union, effectual
calling, and the sacraments. All of these facets, however, can
be subsumed under one or more of the categories in our presen-
tation. For example, mystical union refers to the spiritual union
between Christ and the believer, which is realized in repentance
and faith. Faith understood as a mystical or experiential knowledge of God actually precedes repentance, whereas faith conceived of as trust or confidence accompanies and follows repentance.[7] Again, it can be said that one begins to seek for
God's help at the moment of baptism (the reference here is to
child baptism) and that a life of repentance is made possible
by the sacrament of Holy Communion.

It can be seen that in our schema salvation is understood as
progressing through a series of interacting stages. We hold that
the person who begins to seek for the help of God has already
been confronted by the Spirit of God, and yet he is not truly
saved (justified) until he repents and believes. Nor is he fully
saved (glorified) until his whole being is permeated with the
perfect love of God. The man who begins to seek for help has
incipient salvation. The man who repents and believes has
present salvation. The man who at the end attains perfection

---

[7] See explanatory note 5.

in love has full or final salvation. We might say that at baptism the doorway to salvation is opened. In daily repentance and faith the fruits of salvation are appropriated. In perfect love (as a permanent state) the plan of salvation is consummated.

It is not wrong to make sense of God's revelation so long as we do not try to explain it away. The revelation is still a mystery. Yet, as Kierkegaard maintained, we should seek to use our reason to show that we cannot understand fully. The evangelic plan, as we have presented it, still remains a mystery. The two orders of salvation, the divine and the temporal, can be brought together only in paradoxical language. This means that the predestined can be properly described only as those who seek for help. The sanctified can be understood only as those who obey. The inverses of these two propositions can also be affirmed and are equally in accord with biblical thinking.

This position must not be confused with synergism. In our view God not only takes the initiative, but He also follows through. Yet man is active also from the beginning to the end. The temporal order describes man's activity; the divine order refers only to God's activity. But it is important to note that man's activity is grounded in God's activity. Predestination is nothing else but divine election through human decision. Yet man's decision rests not on free will but rather on free grace. From our side the decision of faith will appear to be, in Barth's words, "a leap into the darkness of the unknown."[8] From the divine side the decision of faith must be viewed in terms of irresistible grace. We are not trying to dissolve the paradox, but rather we are letting the paradox remain a paradox.

The view presented here is not only paradoxical but also dialectical. It attempts to hold together the objective and subjective poles of our salvation. The synthesis is only in the future. Now we must walk by faith. It must be said that the dialectic that we envisage involves Christ and the new man, not the old man. The dialectical engagement takes place be-

---

[8] Karl Barth, *The Epistle to the Romans,* trans. from the sixth edition by Edwin C. Hoskyns (London: Oxford University Press, 1933), p. 98. Barth has become much more cautious in speaking of faith as a "leap."

tween Christ and the man in whom the Holy Spirit dwells. The
Holy Spirit must be viewed as being the only point of contact
between Christ and man. Otherwise we would again be back in
the morass of synergism and Pelagianism.

This view can also be considered dynamic. It seeks to relate
the work on the cross to concrete human experience. We have
not died with Christ unless we live with Him in the complexi-
ties and agonies of the world about us. We have not risen with
Christ unless we suffer with Him in this same world. That is to
say, there is a definite correlation between the objective efficacy
and the subjective evidence of our redemption.

What are the theological implications of this position, which
might be described as a biblical, dynamic view? First of all, the
foundation of our salvation is Jesus Christ Himself, and not a
secret or hidden decree of God. This must be insisted upon
against that strand of Reformed orthodoxy that separates the
decree of God from the redemption of Christ. Again, the reality
of salvation can be affirmed only for those who have faith. Here
one can discern a marked difference from Karl Barth's position.
We can also say in contradistinction to Calvin that faith is not
a mere instrument of salvation but a precondition of salvation.

The most significant implication is that the Christian life is
the arena of salvation. It is the battlefield on which our salvation is fought for and secured. To be sure, in one sense we
can also regard the life and death of Jesus Christ as the arena
of redemption. But in the context of this discussion it is better
to refer to the work of Christ as the foundation of salvation —
meaning here not simply the starting point but the ground or
objective reality of our salvation. The Christian life must be
viewed as being organically related to and rooted in this other
crucial sphere of action. At the same time the Christian life
must be recognized as being equally indispensable for our salvation.

The position taken here will become clearer after a perusal
of the theological implications of the classical Reformed view
of salvation. In that view we find the doctrine of limited atonement and a marked stress on the extrinsic character of justifica-

tion.[9] The foundation of salvation is held to be a secret decree of God.[10] The Christian life is conceived primarily as an effect or fruit of salvation rather than a vital contributing factor in our salvation. Occasionally the biblical idea reasserts itself that good works are the divinely appointed road by which we are to attain eternal life. Yet the predominant emphasis is on works as a sign and confirmation of our eternal election. The struggle to remain true to our faith is not treated seriously, since according to this point of view election and salvation are predetermined. In our view the fruit is organically related to the root. Moreover, the absence of fruit can imperil the very life of faith itself. If we say that the Christian life contributes to our salvation, this actually means that the Holy Spirit contributes to our salvation. The truly good works of the Christian are nothing but the fruits of the Holy Spirit.

There have been some bold attempts within Protestantism to reclaim the role of the Christian life in our salvation. The German Pietists rightly saw that salvation is not only something done for man but also something done in man. They properly discerned the integral relationship between sound thinking and repentance and obedience. Yet the Pietist movement, particularly in its later phases, lost sight of the fact that

---

[9] For a contemporary criticism of Reformed scholastic speculation concerning extrinsic justification or "justification from eternity" see G. C. Berkouwer, *Faith and Justification,* trans. Lewis Smedes (Grand Rapids: Wm. B. Eerdmans, 1954), pp. 143-168. Berkouwer, who seeks to restate the Reformed position on this matter, contends that although justification has its ground in God's eternal election revealed in Christ, it is realized in time only in faith. Berkouwer holds to the essential correlation between justification and faith against all extreme forms of objectivism and subjectivism. He retains, however, the older Reformed idea that once we have faith we cannot totally fall from it. At the same time he rightly warns against holding to perseverance without seeking always to continue in faith. See his *Faith and Perseverance,* trans. Robert Knudsen (Grand Rapids: Wm. B. Eerdmans, 1958).

[10] In the words of one Reformed confession: "That some receive the gift of faith from God, and others do not receive it, proceeds from God's eternal decree. . . . Therefore election is the fountain of every saving good; from which proceed faith, holiness, and the other gifts of salvation, and finally eternal life itself, as its fruits and effects. . . ." Canons of the Synod of Dort. Section I, Arts. VI, IX. In Philip Schaff, ed., *The Creeds of Christendom,* III, pp. 582, 583. Cf. The Westminster Confession, Ch. III.

only Christ lives the authentic Christian life. Only He is the
sanctified man and the "new man" in the full sense of these
words.

It must be recognized that Philip Jacob Spener, the founder
of Pietism, was very much aware of the perils of perfectionism
and pointed to the need of an ever more perfect obedience on
the part of the Christian. At the same time he tended to conceive of regeneration as something consummated in a single
moment rather than a lifelong process. As a result, he did
not do justice to the fact that the Christian is always in a state
of sin as well as in a state of grace. In Spener's thinking a
Christian who has fallen stands in need of a new regeneration
or conversion. We would say that the fallen-away Christian
after acknowledging his sin must resume the struggle towards
full regeneration. The Pietist emphasis is on the "joys of the
heart" and the possession of salvation; our emphasis is on a
life of sacrifice and perseverance.

A parallel movement to German Pietism was English Puritanism, which also sought to reclaim the role of the Christian
life in our salvation. Both movements emphasized the inner life
and practical devotion, but the Puritans were much more icono-
clastic regarding the inherited forms of worship and also much
less removed from the political life of their times. The Puritans
placed the emphasis on the need to confirm our election by
works of piety, but they did not take seriously the biblical truth
that it is possible to forfeit divine election and salvation.

Eighteenth-century Evangelicalism in England and America
shared a similar concern for the Christian life, with the emphasis now being on a crisis experience of conversion. Especially
in the Methodist wing of this movement, however, the doorway
was opened to perfectionism. This took the form of the doctrine of "entire sanctification" or "the second blessing," which
came to characterize much of later revivalism. It must be acknowledged that Wesley himself, although he affirmed the possibility of perfect love, held that the Christian is never wholly
free from transgressions and that even the sanctified therefore
need to repent.

The principal contention of this chapter is that there is a

divine evangelic plan, but that it can be only partially known. There are two poles or perspectives of salvation, an eternal and a temporal, and these poles must be held together in dialectical tension. The design of salvation is manifested to the world in Christ, but it is made effectual in the world only through the spiritual struggles of the faithful. The purposes of God will not be consummated until the old man has been totally crucified and the man of faith totally sanctified. This will not happen for the whole church until the second advent of Jesus Christ. To ascertain the full meaning of salvation we must look backward to Calvary; but if we would partake of the full benefits of salvation, then we must look forward to glory.

II

The Various Meanings of Salvation

In the Bible how to be saved means basically how to be "in the right" before a God who is absolutely holy and righteous. Man was created for covenantal fellowship with God, but this fellowship has been sundered through sin. Salvation in its deepest sense refers to the rectifying or restoration of the broken relationship between God and man, a restoration which entails a transformation of the being of man. The message of the Bible is that God has done for us what we cannot do for ourselves. He has taken the guilt and punishment due to sin upon Himself so that His children might be restored to fellowship with Him. His gratuitous love was nowhere more powerfully expressed than in the vicarious suffering of His Son Jesus Christ on Calvary, although this love was already very much manifest in the prior history of Israel.

In the Old Testament the redemptive action of God is very often expressed in terms of His gracious renewal of the covenant with His people despite their perpetual failings. The ground of the covenantal relationship is God's merciful righteousness and steadfast love (*chesed*). Man's responsibility in the covenantal relationship is heartfelt repentance and faithfulness. But God's righteousness cannot be earned or merited, since man's faithfulness is forever imperfect (Ps. 130:3; 143:2; Is. 64:6). God accounts His children righteous out of His boundless compassion (Is. 53:11; Mic. 7:18). Man can be righteous or stand in a right relationship with God only through grace. Yet man can lose the righteousness and favor of God through idolatry and injustice. In the Psalms and Second Isaiah salvation (*yecha*) and righteousness are practically identical terms (cf. Ps. 71:15; 98:2; Is. 51:5-11; 59:17; 61:10). Salvation can also refer to the concrete effects of God's righteousness and compassion, namely, health, victory, prosperity, and happiness. Yet these fruits of salvation are always seen as being related to and grounded in the righteousness and loving-kindness of God.

The connection between salvation and righteousness can also be discerned in the New Testament. Salvation (*soteria*) is often depicted in terms of the kingdom of God and His righteousness (Mt. 6:33; Rom. 14:17). Paul in particular links salvation and righteousness very closely (Rom. 1:16f.; Phil. 3:8f.). But salvation also has more restricted meanings in the New Testament. It frequently refers specifically to glorification (I Pet. 1:5; I Thes. 5:9; II Tim. 2:10). Sometimes salvation is expressly distinguished from justification, the righteousness accounted to us by faith (Rom. 5:9, 10; Heb. 9:25-28). But in other places salvation appears to include justification (Rom. 10:9, 10; Tit. 3:4-7).

In the history of the church salvation has been given a very broad meaning, and has been made to encompass the whole process of God's justifying and liberating work from the incarnation to the second advent. It has already been shown in the preceding chapter that salvation in its broadest sense can be said to have four facets or dimensions. These can be listed as election, justification, sanctification, and perfection or glorification. We have seen how each of these facets of salvation has both an eternal ground and a basis in history. It was also recognized that each facet is related to the subjective experience of the believer as well as to the objective work of God in Jesus Christ.

Election and predestination are the foundational categories in the schema of salvation. These words are not identical in their root meanings, but in the history of theology they have both come to refer to the eternal decision of God to justify and redeem His children. But this decision must not be separated from His redemptive action in Jesus Christ. Neither can it be disjoined from the work of the Holy Spirit in our lives. Election (*ekloge*) leads *to* and takes place *in* the incarnation of Christ. Election is completed in the effectual calling and transformation of sinners by the Holy Spirit (Rom. 8:29, 30). What God decides, He declares, and what He declares, He does. The Hebrew word *dabar* signifies both the word of God and the act of God. God's election is not only a decree; it is also a process that is organically related to the events of sacred history and to religious experience and obedience. Unless election is viewed in this way there is a danger of falling into a metaphysical determinism.

One problem that has proved particularly troublesome in the history of theology is the relation between justification and sanctification. Emil Brunner holds that these words are metaphors that describe different aspects of the same event. Arthur Crabtree in his work *The Restored Relationship* makes a similar judgment, maintaining that justification and sanctification are parallel terms that express the restorative and transforming action of God from different perspectives. Justification, he contends, is a regal-legal word signifying a change of relationship from condemnation to acquittal; sanctification is a cultic word and describes the redemptive act in terms of a transition from the profane to the holy.[1]

The tendency to view justification and sanctification as parallel terms referring to different aspects of the Christ-event undercuts the biblical insight that there is an order of salvation. Salvation is not simply an event or act but a process or movement which has a beginning and an end. Moreover, the Scriptures speak of different levels and stages in the salvific movement (cf. Is. 42:5-16; Rom. 8:29, 30; Gal. 4:4-6; II Thes. 2:13, 14). To be sure, these stages are inseparable from the total act of salvation, which has yet to be realized in its entirety. Again, it must be recognized that justification in the Pauline epistles roughly corresponds to sanctification in some other New Testament writings (cf. Rom. 5:1, 2; Jn. 17:17-19; Heb. 10:10-14). Yet Paul himself was careful to distinguish between these two dimensions of the salvific process (Rom. 5:9; 6:19, 22).

Both [margin annotation]

---

1 Arthur Crabtree, *The Restored Relationship* (Valley Forge, Pa.: Judson Press, 1963), pp. 165, 186.

Calvin thought of justification and sanctification as being complementary rather than parallel terms. One reason for his view was that unless justification in its forensic aspect is clearly distinguished from sanctification in its ethical aspect, the way is open to works-righteousness. Calvin rightly discerned that the theologian has to do more than simply uncover the original meaning of biblical words; he must also sharpen and rephrase word-meanings in the light of the theological discussion in the history of the church, so that every facet of the message of salvation is made as clear as possible.

It might be well for us to examine more closely the subtle relationship between justification and sanctification. Justification in the New Testament primarily refers to a change in the status of man in his relationship to God. Its foundational meaning is forensic as can be seen in an analysis of the words *dikaioun* (to justify) and *dikaiosis* (justification). The imagery is taken from a court of law where the guilty party is declared innocent. Legal symbolism concerning the justification of God is also found in the Old Testament (cf. Ps. 103:6-14; Is. 43:26; 45:21-23; Mic. 7:9, 18). The principal meaning of justification is consequently the forgiveness of sins. Justification is being accepted by God despite the fact that we are unacceptable (Tillich).

But there is also a dynamic element in justification. God not only declares the sinner righteous; he also makes the sinner righteous. Righteousness is not only imputed but also imparted. Justification in the sense of pardon leads into and includes sanctification in the sense of inward cleansing and healing. The word *dikaiosune* can be made to refer to both justification and the transforming power of God. *Dikaiosune* is "both the righteousness which acquits the sinner and the life-force which breaks the bondage of sin."[2] In the preceding chapter it was pointed out that the prior terms in our picture of the plan of salvation include the others. Justification certainly is organically connected with the inward transformation which is fulfilled in final perfection. Yet it is better to separate justi-

[2] Gottfried Quell and Gottlob Schrenk, *Righteousness* (London: Adam & Charles Black, 1951), p. 53.

fication in its legal aspect from sanctification in its ethical dimension for purposes of clarification. Justification, even in the sense of *dikaiosune,* has an unmistakably legal character, and it would result in a serious distortion of the biblical message if this term were confused with sanctification.

What then is sanctification? Sanctification (*hagiasmos, hagiazein*) has both cultic and ethical connotations. It signifies the act of God by which He separates His people for consecrated service and sets them in opposition to sin. This act by which man is separated from that which is profane involves inward cleansing and purification. Sanctification is therefore closely related to regeneration, liberation, and healing. In its subjective dimension it refers to the cleansing and transforming that the Holy Spirit accomplishes within the believer. Whereas justification represents primarily a change of status, sanctification refers to a change in being. Justification means to be covered by the righteousness of Christ; sanctification means to be engrafted into this righteousness.

Yet it must be recognized that although justification and sanctification are to be distinguished, they must not be separated. Justification and sanctification are two sides of the redemptive action of God. Hans Küng refers to these realities as "two steps" in the process of salvation.[3] Justification is, of course, logically prior to sanctification. The declaration of righteousness logically precedes the impartation of righteousness, but they actually happen simultaneously. Calvin likened justification and sanctification to the light and heat of the sun respectively.[4] These two facets of salvation occur together, but justification is the ground of sanctification. Another way to state this is that the ground of our salvation is simply the mercy and vindication of God and not the disposition towards holiness that is implanted within man. Schleiermacher was in serious error when he made the remission of sins contingent upon the sanctifica-

---

[3] See explanatory note 6.
[4] Calvin, *Institutes of the Christian Religion,* ed. John McNeill, trans. Ford Lewis Battles (Philadelphia: Westminster Press, 1960), III, 11, 6, p. 732.

tion of man.[5] We must never lose sight of the truth that God justifies the *ungodly* (Rom. 4:5; 5:6) or that Christ died for us while we were yet *sinners* (Rom. 5:8).

It must be borne in mind that sanctification, like justification, has its objective basis in the Christ of history. But both realities are subjectively realized by the Holy Spirit in the believer. The verdict of our acquittal and also the power to live a new life must be appropriated by the sinner if he is to become free of sin *de facto*. He receives this verdict by faith; the transforming power becomes operative in his life through love. The experience of faith initially unites us to Christ, but this union is perfected by lifelong fidelity and love. This means that justification is itself fulfilled in the sanctification of the believer. In the deepest sense we are justified only by grace; but we are justified *in* faith and *for* obedience and sanctity. Extrinsic justification must therefore give rise to concrete justification or sanctification if it is to have lasting efficacy.

The term "regeneration" (*palingenesia*) is usually linked with sanctification rather than justification. The word is found only twice in the New Testament (Mt. 19:28; Tit. 3:5). Related terms such as "the new birth" and "birth from above" also are not too prevalent. Yet in the history of theology "regeneration" is a quite common expression. Calvin includes sanctification within regeneration. Louis Berkhof makes sanctification the more inclusive term. Wesley identifies regeneration with the experience of the new birth and sanctification with the experience of perfect love. In Tillich's theology regeneration signifies "participation in the New Being" and sanctification "transformation by the New Being."[6] Tillich contends that regeneration must be held to accompany justification or else faith be-

---

[5] Friedrich Schleiermacher, *The Christian Faith*, ed. H. R. Mackintosh and J. S. Stewart (Edinburgh: T. & T. Clark, 1928), pp. 455, 480. Roman Catholic scholastic theology has also made the remission of sins dependent on infused grace or implanted holiness. For a recent statement on this see Canon F. Cuttaz, *Our Life of Grace*, trans. Angeline Bouchard (Chicago: Fides Publishers Association, 1958). Cuttaz holds (in line with Thomas Aquinas) that the infusion of grace is the cause and ground of the remission of sins. See pp. 106, 110, 119.

[6] Paul Tillich, *Systematic Theology*, Vol. II (Chicago: University of Chicago Press, 1957), pp. 176-180.

comes a barren intellectualism (as in Melanchthon's theology).
There are many other terms associated with various aspects
of the act of salvation. "Reconciliation," a word belonging to
the imagery of home and family, essentially means the restoration of the broken relationship between the Heavenly Father
and His children. It is linked much more closely with justification than sanctification. "Redemption," taken from the imagery
of the slave-market, means to buy back or redeem from slavery.
It has very close connections with justification (cf. Gal. 3:13;
Eph. 1:7; Col. 1:14). It is also sometimes identified with glorification (Lk. 21:28; Rom. 8:23; Eph. 4:30). In many theologies
it is practically equivalent with salvation itself. "Atonement"
signifies the reparation that satisfies the justice of God. It is
closely related both to "expiation" (the covering over of sin) and
"propitiation" (the pacification of the wrath of God). All these
terms can be subsumed under the categories of justification and
reconciliation.

"The remission of sins" usually refers to justification in its
forensic aspect. In the theology of Thomas Aquinas the remission of sins means not only forgiveness but also the expulsion
of sin. "Adoption" refers to our entrance into the family of
God, and in the New Testament is associated with liberation
(Gal. 4:5; Rom. 8:15) and also glorification (Rom. 8:23).
"Mystical union" signifies the union of the believer and the
indwelling Christ, and is naturally linked with regeneration
and sanctification. "The resurrection of the dead" in the New
Testament refers to our present inward transformation as well
as to the final resurrection of the body (cf. Rom. 6:11; 8:11;
Col. 2:12; Eph. 2:4-6; Phil. 3:10, 11). The term "eternal life"
has practically the same meanings.

A special word should perhaps be said about glorification,
since this is one of the dominant categories in our schema.
In the mind of the church glorification is related to every other
facet of salvation, inasmuch as it represents the culmination of
the salvific process. Glorification refers basically to the state of
eternal bliss in the world to come (Rom. 8:18, 30; II Cor. 4:17;
II Tim. 2:10). It signals the complete rectifying of the broken
relationship between God and man. It represents what Wesley

called "absolute perfection." It also can be equated with "final justification" and "entire sanctification."[7] Roman Catholic mystical theology speaks of "the beatific vision of God." Reformation thought associates the goal of the Christian life with "the crown of holiness" and "the crown of glory." To a limited extent the Christian can already enter into the splendor of the world to come (II Cor. 3:18; I Pet. 4:14; 5:1), and yet this splendor or perfection will always be in this life more of a vision than a possession, a momentary experience rather than a continuous state (Eph. 1:13, 14; Phil. 3:12).

One other basic meaning of salvation that should be considered is healing. Some theologians, among them Paul Tillich and John Baillie, contend that this is the fundamental meaning of salvation. In the Old Testament health is closely associated with the salvation (*yecha*) and peace (*shalom*) of God. Jeremiah exclaims: "Heal me, O Lord, and I shall be healed; save me, and I shall be saved" (Jer. 17:14; cf. 30:17). The restoration of the relationship between God and man that was broken by sin is often depicted in terms of healing (cf. Ps. 41:4; Is. 58:8). Health is not discussed in medical terms in the Old Testament but always in religious terms. Just as sickness is often associated with the condemnation of God (cf. Num. 12:10; II Chr. 21:11-19), so health is related directly to the salvation of God.

There is an even more intimate association between salvation and health in the New Testament. The Greek word for salvation (*soteria*) in extra-biblical usage meant primarily the bodily health that follows a recovery from illness. It also referred to deliverance from every kind of calamity. In the New Testament the meaning is extended to signify total recovery and release from the disease of sin. The Vulgate translates *soteria* with the Latin *salus,* the root meaning of which is definitely health and well-being. The English word "salvation" is derived from *salus.*

To interpret salvation as the healing of the body and soul places the accent on transformation and sanctification. This is a legitimate interpretation, but it must not be emphasized to

[7] See explanatory note 7.

the exclusion of other facets of the salvific process. As we have seen, salvation involves a change of status as well as a change of being. God not only heals the sinner of his infirmities but also forgives his iniquities (Ps. 103:3). Moreover, we must bear in mind that although we are fully forgiven (and healed) in Jesus Christ, our personal or actual healing is only partial, since vestiges of sin remain within us until the resurrection to glory. We can say that one is not *fully* saved (perfected) without being completely well. At the same time we must acknowledge that one may be *truly* saved (justified) and yet be sick.

Does salvation mean the healing of the body and mind as well as the soul or inner self? This question leads to a consideration of the relation between salvation in its theological context and its various cultural meanings. The deliverance of man in the Old Testament often includes the healing of bodily ailments (cf. Ps. 107:17-20; Prov. 3:7, 8). In the New Testament also salvation is associated with recovery from bodily diseases. It is interesting to note that the word *sozein* (to save) is used for Jesus' healing of the blind man (Mk. 10:52), His curing of the leper (Lk. 17:19), and His healing of the woman with a hemorrhage (Mt. 9:22). It is also significant that it is in answer to the question on his healing of a cripple that Peter points to Jesus Christ as the only name under heaven by which we must be saved (Acts 4:7-12).

Yet one must take care in seeking to correlate the theological meaning or meanings of salvation and the cultural or philosophical understanding of this term.[8] Salvation cannot mean the very same to the believer who trusts in the mercy of God and to the secular psychologist or philosopher who has only a confused perception of the reality of sin. This is why the term "catharsis," as used by psychotherapists, is not identical with the theological term "forgiveness." There may very well be a wide disparity between such socio-psychological terms as "integration" and "humanization" and what we have defined as sanctification. What the social worker understands by "rehabilitation" will be somewhat different from regeneration in its biblical usage. Rehabilita-

8 See explanatory note 8.

tion into society may or may not be a sign of deeper change in the individual, but there is no necessary causal connection between the two phenomena. Certainly salvation would tend to exclude full rehabilitation into an atheistic or avowedly non-Christian society. On the other hand, salvation might very well include rehabilitation into a society where Christian values are normative. Recovery from an illness may be a step towards conversion in its biblical sense, or it may have little to do with conversion. Only one of the lepers who were healed returned to praise Jesus (Lk. 17:11f.). And, of course, the cultural understanding of freedom is not the same as Christian liberty. One can have intellectual and cultural freedoms but still remain enslaved to sin. One can even be free from pathological anxiety and yet be afflicted with "hardness of heart."

At the same time, we must affirm that the theological meaning of salvation is certainly related to the cultural meanings. The saving grace of Christ both fulfills and negates natural needs and desires. Physical and emotional health is certainly a sign of the resurrection of the body, even where unbelievers are involved. Freedom from physical slavery points to the deeper inward freedom from slavery to sin that Christ desires for all men. Since salvation in the theological sense entails the renovation and transformation of the whole man, the healing of any area of the personality or body of man is an anticipation of that final goal (*telos*) when man shall have an immortal soul and an incorruptible body. To be sure, the body of man must finally decay because sin is not fully eradicated in the forgiven sinner. But the inner man is being continually renewed, and it is this inner man who will finally triumph over death. Moreover, the Christian has the assurance that his earthly body will share in this triumph by being resurrected on the last day (Jn. 6:40; Rom. 8:23).

The Bible not only speaks of four basic categories in the area of soteriology, but also of three basic tenses — past, present, and future. To be sure, there are variations within these tenses. In the Greek there are four separate tenses for the past dimension of time alone. All of the various categories or facets of salvation can be found in past, present, and future. A study of such words as *sozein* (to save), *dikaioun* (to justify), and *hagia-zein* (to sanctify) makes this very clear.

When we say that our salvation takes place in the past, we have in mind God's election of man in Christ before the world (cf. Eph. 1:4; II Thes. 2:13). We also must look to God's deliverance of Israel from Egypt and His providential care of His people in the wilderness. But, above all, we must fix our attention on the life and death of Jesus Christ, since the decree of God is made final in the incarnation of His Son. God's decree is not secret because it is made known decisively and fully in the person and work of Jesus Christ.

But salvation also takes place in the present. The election of God is being realized now in our lives through the Holy Spirit. It is not only the perfected life of Christ in the past but the faithful life of the believer in the present that makes salvation effectual. It is not only Christ's death on the cross but the bearing of the cross by the people of the church that prepares the way for ultimate victory.

Thirdly, of course, salvation has a future or eschatological aspect. Here we are thinking of perfection in the kingdom beyond history. Salvation in the future signals our final justification and eternal life with the saints in glory. Paul refers to this culmination of salvation when he says that "we ourselves, who have the first fruits of the Spirit, groan inwardly as we wait for adoption as sons, the redemption of our bodies" (Rom. 8:23).

The three sides or tenses of salvation are particularly evident in the words of Paul concerning the institution of the Lord's Supper: "For as often as you eat this bread and drink the cup, you proclaim the Lord's death until he comes" (I Cor. 11:26). Here we can see past, present, and future tied together in an organic, but at the same time mysterious, unity. The Holy Supper is not only an effectual sign of the historical deliverance on the cross, but also of the visitation of Christ in the present and His final triumph in the future.

Not only salvation itself, but every facet of salvation participates in all three dimensions of time. Election, justification, sanctification, and perfection are all to be found in past, present, and future. To be sure, the meanings of these words vary considerably from one tense to another. Justification in the past refers to the remission of sins; justification in the future signifies a purgatorial judgment and final cleansing on the basis of faithful works (Mt. 12:36, 37; Rom. 2:6-13; I Cor. 3:13-15). Perfection in the future signifies inward personal transformation. We might say that the seed of perfection is in the past, its germination occurs in the present, and the flower of perfection is in the future.

Moreover, every category of salvation is organically related to every other. We can affirm that our election is not complete until our glorification. The meaning here is that the fruits of our election in Christ are not fully appropriated until final or total sanctification. We can also hold that we are not fully justified until we are perfected. In spite of Luther's stress upon the forensic and past aspects of justification he could write: "For God has not yet justified us, i.e., he has not yet made us perfectly righteous and our righteousness complete, but he has begun to perfect it. . . ."[9]

Predestination has been very much misunderstood because it has not been viewed in the context of the three dimensions of time. Very often we think of predestination as occurring only in the past. Its root meaning, of course, does basically refer to the past. Yet we forget that it also has a present and a future side. Its foundation is in the past, but its realization is in the present and its consummation in the future. The future is open. God's plan of salvation is, of course, perfected concerning the broad outlines of the advancement and consummation of the kingdom. But the particulars in the realization of this plan have not yet been determined. This is why predestination is both something that is final and also something that has yet to be realized. Barth has written: "God's predestination . . . is not an exhausted work, a work which is behind us. On the contrary, it is a work which still takes place in all its fullness today."[10] It is in the light of this truth that we can understand

9 See explanatory note 9.
10 Karl Barth, *Church Dogmatics*, II, 2, ed. G. W. Bromiley & T. F. Torrance, trans. G. W. Bromiley, *et al.* (Edinburgh: T. & T. Clark, 1957), p. 183.

Staupitz's advice to the tormented Luther as the latter struggled with doubts about his election: if one would but cling to Christ he would then be predestined. Luther later gave similar counsel to a woman who was afflicted with the same anxiety: "Hear the Incarnate Son, He freely offers thee himself as Predestination."[11] Predestination is to be associated not with automatic salvation or damnation but with the invitation to pilgrimage and faith.

This brings us to the terrifying conception of double predestination. In contradistinction to the older Reformed theology we do not affirm a double predestination in the sense that some men are automatically excluded from salvation even before they hear the gospel message. It is more biblical to speak of a single predestination to life and service for all men. But we must not suppose that this predestination is realized in the same way for every person. For believers it is realized in their adoption to sonship in the kingdom of heaven. For unbelievers it is realized in their subjugation as servants of the heavenly king. If predestination is to issue in the fullness of life, faith is necessary.

Finally, it must be recognized that salvation is both an objective accomplishment and a subjective decision. It is a gift and a task at the same time. These two poles are to be found also in every facet of salvation. Paul proclaims that our sanctification has been made actual in Christ (I Cor. 1:30), but he also pleads with his hearers to sanctify themselves (II Cor. 7:1; Rom. 12:1). The writer of I John holds that we have been cleansed of sin at the new birth (I Jn. 3:9), but at the same time he urges the Christian community to purify themselves (3:3). The Scriptures never speak of self-justification except as something to be condemned; rather, we are called to believe and obey. We are justified by Christ, but also by our acceptance of Christ (Gal. 3:24). Even the obedience of the Christian plays a role in his justification (in regard to the appropriation of the fruits of justification) (cf. Jas. 2:24; I Jn. 3:7). We cannot elect ourselves to salvation, but it is incumbent upon us to confirm our election and make it sure (II Pet. 1:10). We are never

11 Quoted in Gordon Rupp, *The Righteousness of God* (London: Hodder & Stoughton, 1963), p. 283.

commanded to glorify ourselves, but we are called to be perfect
(Lev. 11:44, 45; Mt. 5:48; Heb. 12:14; I Pet. 1:15, 16).

In summary, salvation predicates the justification and restoration of the whole man. It entails the healing not only of the
spirit of man but also of his mind and body (I Thes. 5:23).
Perfect love, which is the consummation of salvation, signifies
perfect wholeness. Total sanctity predicates the fullness of maturity and complete sanity. Salvation involves the conversion
not only of our attitudes to God and man but also of our attitudes to society. To become a new man means to become a
different person in the social and economic spheres of life as well
as in the religious sphere. The Iona Community lays much
stress upon "whole salvation" as over against "soul salvation."
But this dichotomy is actually misleading, since in the New
Testament the salvation of the *soul* (Mt. 16:26; I Pet. 1:9;
Jas. 5:20) means the salvation of the whole man.

The kingdom of God signifies not only the salvation of the
individual but preëminently the salvation of the people of God.
The goal of Christian faith is something more than personal holiness; it is none other than a holy community (cf. Calvin).
It is a new social order in which the sacred and secular are
brought into a creative synthesis. This new society is present
now to a certain degree within the fellowship of believers, but
it will not be realized in its fullness within the sphere of earthly
history. The consummation of God's plan of salvation lies
beyond history.[12]

12 See explanatory note 10.

III

The Divine Sacrifice

Holy Scripture clearly teaches that the Christian life is grounded in the death and resurrection of Jesus Christ. That the Christian life is anchored in an objective unrepeatable event in world history certainly merits emphasis in a period, such as ours, when the absolute character and finality of the Christian revelation are being called into question by Christian existentialists, who subjectivize and psychologize the events of salvation, and by process theologians (such as Wieman and Ogden), who relativize these events.[1] Salvation has both an objective and a subjective pole, but it must be emphasized that the objective pole is prior and indeed basic to the subjective response that constitutes the Christian life. The foundation of the Christian life is not an existential decision nor a mystical experience but the decisive, irrevocable work of God in the sacrificial life and death of Jesus Christ. In one sense, we can affirm that our salvation has its beginning not in the moment of decision (although such a decision is indispensable for our salvation) but rather on the mount of Calvary.

Paul traced the objective ground of salvation beyond history to eternity. He stated that before he was born he was set apart for salvation (Gal. 1:15). The prophet Jeremiah voiced a similar conviction: "Before I formed you in the womb I knew you, and before you were born I consecrated you" (Jer. 1:5). Classical theology has rightly discerned that the mystery of sal-

---

[1] See explanatory note 11.

vation is hidden in the counsels of God. Calvin (and also Luther) spoke of a decree in the mind of God before the foundation of the world. It is certainly proper to posit such a decree, but we must affirm, against Calvinist orthodoxy, that this decree is not secret but is truly revealed in Jesus Christ. The gracious purpose of God has been fully manifest in the appearance of Christ on earth (II Tim. 1:9, 10). Since our salvation is anchored in Christ, its foundation is both eternal and historical, for Christ is true God and true man. The sign of our election is consequently the cross of Calvary. We are elected before the creation of the world, but we are elected *in* Christ (Eph. 1:4; cf. I Pet. 1:20). Calvin himself affirmed:

> Since the certainty of salvation is set forth to us in Christ, it is wrong and injurious to Christ to pass over this proffered fountain of life from which supplies are available, and to toil to draw life out of the hidden recesses of God. Paul testifies indeed that we were chosen before the foundation of the world; but, he adds, in Christ (Eph. 1:4). Let no one then seek confidence in his election elsewhere, unless he wish to obliterate his name from the book of life in which it is written.[2]

When we speak of the life of the Christian as being anchored in the death on the cross, we have in mind of course more than simply the crucifixion of Jesus. The death on the cross signifies the dying of Jesus in the context of His whole life and also as related to His resurrection. Calvary is a symbol not only of the crucifixion but of the Christ-event, which includes His life, death, and resurrection. The conquering death of Jesus was but the fulfillment of His sinless life and the basis of His resurrection triumph.

To affirm that our salvation is rooted in Christ means to hold that this salvation is grounded not only in the work of God but also in the work of man. To be sure, God accomplished and effectuated our reconciliation in Christ, but He did this through the obedience of the man Jesus (Rom. 5:19; Phil. 2:8). In Jesus Christ we see both God and the Mediator between God and man. Jesus can be regarded as the mirror and sign

2 John Calvin, *Concerning the Eternal Predestination of God*, trans. J. K. S. Reid (London: James Clarke & Co., Ltd., 1961), p. 126.

of God transcendent. He is also to be viewed as the working partner of God immanent. If our salvation is described as a past event, we must have in mind not only God's decisive work in Christ at Calvary but also the bearing of the cross by Jesus. It is possible to hold that our justification was actualized both objectively and subjectively in Jesus Christ, since Jesus the man fulfilled His role as sacrificial victim. What took place in Jesus is both justification as the objective act of the redeeming God and the subjective realization of it in our torn humanity. The past event of salvation includes therefore not only *agape,* the sacrificial love of God to man, but also *eros,* the aspiring love of the man Jesus. But this is an *eros* untainted by sin and united with *agape.* The past event of salvation must be understood in terms of the paradox of the election and obedience of Jesus Christ. He was elected for obedience, but His election was realized and fulfilled only in His obedience. The author of our salvation is the holy God, but the medium of our salvation is the holy humanity of Jesus. The sacrifice on the cross is therefore not simply a divine sacrifice but a divine-human sacrifice.

The sacrifice of Christ must be understood against the background of the plight of man who is lost. The dilemma of man is that, having been created in the image of God, he has marred this image by seeking his own glory and has become enslaved to his self-seeking will. In the language of the Bible, man's dilemma is that he is lost in sin. Sin, as envisaged by biblical faith, is both an act and a state. It is an act of rebellion against the holy God and a state of bondage to the driving power of this rebellion. The act of sin produces an aberrant desire or weakness that some theologians have called "the tinder of sin." This tinder of sin might be understood as a propensity to evil, a propensity inherent in the human race. It is not to be conceived as a deficiency or privation, but rather as a positive inclination to evil. It is not simply lust or concupiscence; rather, it is a lust for power. Actual sins are the fruits of the tinder of sin.

The fact that sin as an act precedes and springs from the tinder of sin points to the mystery of original sin. This mystery reminds us that sin proceeds not only from man but also to man. Even before the human race this propensity to evil existed. Classical theologians have tried to explain it by the myth of the fallen angels. This, however, is not an explanation but simply a partial illumination of something that is basically mysterious and inexplicable. The fact of the matter is that sin cannot be explained to our own satisfaction, for then it could be excused. Barth calls sin an "ontological impossibility." Sin is not willed by God but excluded from His creation. Yet it happens out of man's inexplicable refusal to let God be God. Sin happens with God's permission and may be occasioned by demonic temptation. Yet man is to be held fully accountable for it, since there is nothing in his created nature that makes him peculiarly vulnerable to sin. It is not man's freedom but the misuse of his freedom that makes him susceptible to sin.

The core of sin is unbelief or hardness of heart. It has been described as *cor curvum in se* (the heart turned in upon itself). A hardened heart is caused by a mixture of rebellion and weakness. But this is a weakness for which man is responsible, a weakness to which he willfully succumbs. This weakness is not part of his created nature but a blot on this nature. Man's weakness must be seen as an element in his rebellion. Yet his rebellion cannot be understood apart from this weakness and indeed is occasioned by it. Only demonic sin can be regarded as sheer rebellion (Emil Brunner).

The two chief manifestations of sin are pride and sensuality or slothfulness. Tillich calls these manifestations *"hubris"* and "concupiscence." Pride refers to the sins of the spirit, and sensuality encompasses the sins of the flesh. Luther referred to the sins of the spirit as "white sins" and the sins of the flesh as "black sins." In his view the "white sins" are always the most virulent, since they afflict the religious man even more than the non-religious man. In fact, Luther says, the closer we grow towards God, the more susceptible we become to the sins of moral and religious pride. The sins of the spirit are the sins of the Pharisee, and it is against these sins that Jesus warned most vehemently.

Reinhold Niebuhr has reminded us that sin has collective as

well as personal dimensions.[3] Nations and races and even religious groups can be guilty of pride as well as individuals. Niebuhr maintains that even though an individual may attain a relative degree of personal or private morality, he nevertheless participates in the sins and injustices of an immoral society and can therefore never be actually blameless in the sight of God. Popular American Protestantism needs to be reminded that there is a collective dimension of sin which reveals itself in injustice and that man by himself is powerless to escape from group sin even though he might make some progress in overcoming personal vices.

In order to discern the full implications of the biblical doctrine of sin, we first must recognize that sin is a state of ignorance. By turning from the source of our existence, we have become blind to God's signs and deaf to His word. As opposed to the Socratic understanding of ignorance, the Christian faith holds that ignorance of God's will is something for which man must be held accountable. The root of ignorance is hardness of heart (Eph. 4:18). We are guilty of ignorance because we seek to hide ourselves from the light. We fear to know the truth about God and ourselves, and therefore like Adam we flee from God. The man who is ignorant of the will of God stands in need of a prophet who will bring him the enlightenment that can set him free.

Sin must also be seen as a state of bondage. By willfully assenting to the temptations that confront us from within and without, we become bound to powers and forces beyond our control. In theological language these powers are identified as "sin, death, and the devil." Sin is not merely something we do but something to which we become enslaved. We become bound not only to the powers of vicious habits and dark and foreboding thoughts but also to the demonic powers of darkness — powers that can be described only in mythical or symbolic language, but which are nevertheless very real. Death is the terrible penalty of sin, and this death must be seen not merely as

[3] See his books *Moral Man and Immoral Society* (New York: Charles Scribner's Sons, 1932) and *An Interpretation of Christian Ethics* (New York: Harper & Bros., 1935).

bodily disintegration but also as separation from the love and presence of God. That is to say, this death has both a physical and an eternal dimension. Those who are in bondage stand in need of liberation and freedom. We seek a Redeemer who will ransom us and fight for us.

Finally, sin must be understood as a state of estrangement. By rebelling against the Creator, we have incurred His displeasure and must be brought before His judgment. The man who transgresses God's law is guilty in God's sight and stands under His wrath. Man's dilemma is that he must pay the penalty which the law demands, but he cannot pay this penalty and still go free. The reason is that sin against an infinite God brings with it an infinite penalty. The penalty for transgression is judgment and hell. The man who is estranged from God therefore stands in dire need of reconciliation with God. He also must be reconciled with his neighbor, since alienation from the ground of being invariably results in alienation from one's fellow-being. He needs a priest who will intercede for him before the throne of God. A sacrifice must be offered for him that will satisfy the justice of God. It must be recognized that guilt is the basic dilemma of fallen man. Because man is guilty, God allows him to fall into blindness and bondage (Is. 42:18f.) .

The glad tidings of the New Testament is that man in sin has been unshackled and declared free by God's incomparable, unrepeatable sacrifice in the person and work of Jesus Christ. The sacrifice of God in Christ, which culminated on the mount of Calvary, is a vicarious sacrifice, since Christ suffered on behalf of others. It is also a substitutionary sacrifice, because He suffered the pains of wrath and hell in our stead. His suffering can be viewed as a propitiation, since it satisfied the wrath of God. It also can be understood as an expiation in that it broke the stranglehold of sin on the lives of men. Finally, it can be considered a penal sacrifice, since Christ took upon Himself the penalty of man's transgression of the divine law, namely, the torments of hell. Yet He suffered not as a doomed sinner but as the loving God. He experienced on the cross not sinful despair but rather the anguish of loving mercy. He was tempted to despair in the Garden of Gethsemane, but this despair was converted into compassion.

One does not grasp the full significance of the sacrifice on Calvary unless he sees this as the suffering not only of the man Jesus but of God Himself. We have affirmed that the humanity of Jesus was integrally involved in this sacrifice. Yet we must now underscore the fact that this humanity was united with deity and that God consequently shared in the tribulations of the humanity of His Son. God suffered in and through the anguish and misery of the dying Jesus. It was not merely a human mediator but God Himself who won the victory for us on the cross. It was God Himself who bore our sin and guilt so that we might go free. We must take care to guard against the modern heresy which makes the suffering of God a matter of metaphysical necessity. It must be recognized that God did not need to suffer, but that He freely willed to suffer in His Son. Suffering is not part of His essential nature; rather, He took suffering upon Himself purely out of His boundless compassion. God is essentially light, but He entered into darkness in the person of His Son so that darkness might be overcome. Yet the mystery of the incarnation is that Christ in His poverty and humiliation remained God and that His weakness was at the same time the power which overthrows the powers of this world.

Since God Himself was intimately involved in the sacrificial living and dying of Jesus, it is possible to speak of two aspects or dimensions of the divine sacrifice. First, there is the self-emptying of God the Son (the *kenosis*), which is equivalent to the incarnation (II Cor. 8:9; Phil. 2:6-8). Second, there is the sacrifice on the cross — the atonement — which signifies the climax and fulfillment of the incarnation. It is thus to be seen that soteriology is grounded in Christology; the cross is inexplicable apart from the incarnation. The paradox of grace and freedom which we find in the life and death of Jesus is a derivative of the "Absolute Paradox," the mystery that God became man in Jesus Christ without ceasing to be God.

The sacrifice of Calvary must be understood not only as a defeat by the world but also as a royal victory over the world. It signifies both the humiliation of Christ and His exaltation, although this exaltation does not become visible to the church except in the resurrection of Christ from the grave. The sacrifice of Christ is a ransom in which He lays down His life for the redemption of man; yet it signifies also a triumph over the powers which control men. Christ was both victor and victim, the Lamb of God who was slain for the sins of the world and the King of glory who triumphed over the power of sin in the world. Besides the crucifix, another potent symbol in the life of the church is the *Christus Rex* — Christ reigning from the cross.

The deepest meaning of Calvary is that Christ suffers not only *for* man but also *as* man — not only on our behalf but also in our place. This is the key to Paul's contention that we were crucified and buried with Him (Rom. 6:1-11; 7:4; cf. II Cor. 5: 14).[4] Jesus Christ is both our Mediator and our Representative. Theodore Hegre cogently points to the deeper significance of the cross: "Had Satan written the inscription, it would have read, 'Jesus of Nazareth, whom I have overcome.' But if God had written the inscription it would have read, 'Here lies the sinful human race.' "[5]

Christ's great work of salvation can be seen to have two principal facets — His work as priest and as king. As priest He performed the one sacrifice that could satisfy divine justice, namely, the offering of a sinless human life on behalf of fallen man. As king He gave His life as a ransom to the powers of darkness on behalf of an enslaved race, but only in order to expose and triumph over the darkness. As priest He procured for us pardon and vindication at the bar of justice; as king He won for us the victory that set us free. His priestly work can be viewed as a propitiation of God's wrath; His kingly work might be seen as an expiation of our sins. That is, Christ not only died for our sins, but He took away our sins. Jesus Christ is both priest and victim, king and slave.

Jesus Christ must also be seen as the prophet who not only

[4] In Paul's mind baptism is the sign of our crucifixion and burial with Christ and also the means by which we become mystically united with His death. Cf. Rom. 6:3, 4; Col. 2:12; Gal. 3:27.

[5] Theodore Hegre, *The Cross and Sanctification* (Minneapolis: Bethany Fellowship Press, 1960), p. 71.

brings truth but incarnates truth. He not only heralds revelation, but He is Himself the revelation. He contains within Himself the truth that can wipe away our ignorance and bring us face to face with ourselves as well as with God. Yet His work as prophet is subordinate to His work as priest and king. His work as Revealer is inseparable from His work as Redeemer. In redeeming us He enlightens us. Our liberation includes our perception of the truth that can make us free. Our reconciliation includes and makes effectual our awakening to the knowledge and love of Jesus Christ. The atonement of Christ is at the same time the revelation of Christ to a world blinded by sin.

Reformation theology has rightly taught that reconciliation involves a mutual concord on the part of God and man. It is not only man's hardness of heart that must be overcome; it is also God's righteous indignation. The message of faith is that in the sacrificial death of Jesus Christ God's wrath has been fully assuaged. His enmity was taken away in the very act of His reconciling the world unto Himself. In Jesus Christ God vindicates Himself as well as the world. He not only declares the world as righteous in Christ but also reveals and proves His righteousness (Rom. 3:26).

It must be borne in mind that the atonement or reconciliation of Christ has two poles — objective and subjective. We here take issue with Anselm, who spoke exclusively in terms of an objective sacrifice that satisfied the justice of God.[6] We also diverge from Aulén, who in his book *Christus Victor* upholds what he terms "the classic theory" of the atonement, in which the atonement is portrayed as a dramatic victory of God over the powers of darkness. There is much truth in this theory, but Aulén insists that this work of reconciliation must be viewed wholly in objectivistic terms — as God's reconciling and redemptive work in the life and death of Jesus Christ. The truth in the moral influence and mystical theories of the atonement is that man needs to be brought into contact in some way

[6] We also object to Anselm's conceiving of the atonement as a purely human sacrifice, an act performed by Jesus as man but not by Jesus as God. See his work *Cur deus homo (Why God Became Man)*, *The Library of Christian Classics*, ed. & trans. Eugene Fairweather (Philadelphia: Westminster Press, 1956), Vol. X, pp. 100-183.

with the redemption of the cross if he is to benefit from this redemption. To be sure, we must not lose sight of the truth that Christ and only Christ is our righteousness and sanctification (I Cor. 1:30). But if this righteousness of Christ is to be effectual in our lives, it must be appropriated by us. His righteousness must be not only imputed to us but also imparted to us. It is true that our salvation is not possible unless Christ is our Representative; yet at the same time He must be the "new man" within us if His atonement is to become a life-giving reality for us. Calvin spoke in terms of a "mystical union" between Christ and the believer. Both Calvin and Luther insisted that we must participate in the atonement just as branches participate in the living vine (cf. Jn. 15:1-11). The crucified and risen Lord alone is the Revealer, but we are channels of His revelation. He alone is the Redeemer, but we are signs and instruments of His redemption. He has purchased our redemption once for all on Calvary, but He wills to make this redemption a vital force in our lives through our faith and love.

This brings us to the truth that the atonement is not only a once-for-all event in history, but that it continues on a new level in the lives of believers. The suffering of Christ on the cross was sufficient for the salvation of the world, but this suffering is not yet fully efficacious in the world. The cross of Christ must be accepted by the world. The saving work of Christ is complete in the sense that the doors to salvation are now opened for all; yet it is incomplete in the sense that not all men have passed through these doors into the kingdom. The priestly work of Christ continues in heaven. His propitiatory sacrifice is finished, but His work as Intercessor will continue until the consummation of the kingdom.

In this connection we must consider the question whether Christ still suffers for the world, inasmuch as the world continues to close its heart to the gospel. Paul tells us in Colossians 1:24 that Christ continues to suffer in His members, but does He suffer in Himself? We must affirm that His agonizing death for sin is finished and cannot be repeated or renewed (cf. Jn. 19:30; Heb. 9:25-28). But His suffering for the salvation of men certainly continues in His role as Intercessor. Did not

Christ reveal to Paul that He felt the persecution against His people (Acts 9:4)? The Epistle to the Hebrews speaks of apostates as crucifying the Son of God anew and putting Him to open shame (Heb. 6:6). In one sense it is possible to speak of the present passion of Christ in that the fruits of His victory have not yet been fully realized. The decisive battle against the principalities and powers has been fought and won, but the war still continues. We are told that Christ will not rest content "until he has put all his enemies under his feet" (I Cor. 15:25).

In speaking of the suffering of Christ on the cross and in the church, we must not fall into the delusion that the members of His church are exempt from suffering. The doctrine of the substitutionary atonement does not mean that Christ alone suffers. To be sure, only His suffering has purchased our redemption, but we have to suffer in bearing witness to this redemption. Christ spares us from the ultimate torments of sin but not from the suffering of faith. He alone is the priest who can offer the one sacrifice that can expiate sin; yet He allows us to intercede and suffer with Him for the salvation of the world (cf. Phil. 1:29; 3:10; II Cor. 1:5, 6; II Tim. 2:10; I Pet. 4:13, 14). Christ alone is our king, but we must fight with Him and for Him. He is the one prophet who incarnates within Himself the truth, but we must bear witness to Him. The Christian needs no longer to suffer as a doomed sinner; he now may suffer as a heroic saint (cf. I Pet. 4:13-16). The suffering of the Christian can be regarded as redemptive suffering insofar as it reveals and communicates the redemption in Christ.

We must remind ourselves that the victory of Christ over sin includes not only the crucifixion but also the resurrection and ascension. These events are simply different facets or stages of the victory of Christ over the powers of darkness. "Calvary" signifies not only the conquering death of Jesus on the cross but His resurrection from the grave and His exaltation at the right hand of God in heaven. The resurrection and ascension both reveal and confirm the power of the cross. The ascension into glory signifies the working out to fulfillment of the victory of the cross and resurrection.

Our position diverges from that held by many contemporary theologians and higher critics concerning the relation of the resurrection and exaltation of Christ. Emil Brunner, for example, contends that the resurrection of Jesus is identical with His exaltation and that the ascension "plays no part in the teaching of the Apostles."[7] It is to be acknowledged that in the apostolic church the resurrection is associated very closely with the exaltation, as Acts 2:32, 33 suggests. Yet it is more true to the total biblical picture to affirm that the cross, the resurrection, and the ascension constitute three separate phases or facets of one movement of redemption. Christ's exaltation has three aspects: crucifixion, resurrection and ascension into glory.

The way to salvation is fundamentally not a series of rationally ascertainable steps to heaven but simply Christ on the cross. We cannot follow His path, but we can follow Him. The way to salvation is first of all a Person and secondarily a life of obedience to this Person. Following the road to Calvary means entering into communion with Christ. To walk this road does not mean a slavish copying of His acts but rather the reproduction of His life in us. To "follow in his steps" (I Pet. 2:21) means to walk in the light of His Word. His historical life is our external norm; His Holy Spirit is our inward guide. The way to salvation is Christ living within us.

The Reformers protested against making the remission of sins contingent on the Christian life (which was the besetting temptation of Roman Catholic theologians), since this opened the door to works-righteousness. The Reformers upheld justification by faith as over against a theology of merit, but they sought to connect this with the obligation to live a righteous life. Yet by placing the locus of reconciliation totally outside the Christian, they were unable to see the Christian life as having any significance beyond being a result or sign of salvation. The Reformers came closest to perceiving the organic relation between the gift of faith and the Christian life in their doctrines of sanctification; yet sanctification never occupied

[7] Emil Brunner, *The Christian Doctrine of Creation and Redemption* (Philadelphia: Westminster, 1949), p. 373.

in their thought the preeminent position accorded to justification.

Certainly it can be argued that Calvin gave a prominent place to sanctification, and his doctrine of progressive sanctification became a dominant motif in sectarian Calvinism and Puritanism. Yet Calvin stressed the fact that the Christian life is a sign or testimony of salvation rather than a means of salvation. Although he discussed regeneration (or sanctification) before justification in his *Institutes,* this does not imply that the former has priority over the latter. On the contrary, he contended that our justification is perfect, whereas our sanctification is rudimentary and incomplete in this life, despite the fact that some progress can be made in the struggle against sin, the flesh, and the devil. Moreover, he was reluctant to affirm that sanctification is the goal of justification, although he recognized their inseparable connection.[8]

In post-Reformation orthodoxy Christian belief became more important than the Christian life, and the call to holiness was pushed very much into the background. Some Lutheran theologians, reacting against the Roman Catholic theology of merit, actually feared an emphasis on good works. Amsdorf went so far as to hold that good works are harmful for salvation. This position was condemned by the Formula of Concord, but nothing positive is to be found in the Formula concerning good works beyond the recognition that such works are a sign or "testimony" of faith (Article IV).

With the Reformers we hold that the basis and source of our salvation is in the past. Yet we insist that the appropriation of salvation is in the present. The Christian life does not purchase salvation, but it is the arena in which our salvation is carried forward to victory. The life of faithful obedience is not simply

---

[8] See Francois Wendel, *Calvin,* trans. Philip Mairet (London: Collins, 1963), p. 56. Although Calvin's basic teaching is that good works are a sign or fruit of our salvation, there are places in his writings where he perceives the Christian life as a contributing factor in our final salvation. For a good summary of Calvin's views on this whole problem see Ronald S. Wallace, *Calvin's Doctrine of the Christian Life* (Grand Rapids: Wm. B. Eerdmans, 1959).

an after-effect of our salvation but a creative element in our salvation.

Contemporary theology is presently divided concerning the locus of the redemption wrought by Christ. Barthian theologians argue that our salvation takes place in the historic Jesus Christ, Christ crucified and risen.[9] Bultmann locates salvation in the existential encounter with the Christ of the kerygma. Clinton Morrison maintains that salvation occurs in the community of believers. He argues that whereas the lordship of Christ is over the whole world, the locus of His victory is the church.[10] Our view is that there are two loci or poles of salvation, the cross of Christ and the obedience of faith. Indeed, it is possible to point to a third locus of salvation, the second advent of Christ, which signifies the climax and consummation of His saving work. Barth himself acknowledges a subjective pole of the atonement, but he regards this as "the unique history of Jesus Christ," which encloses and exemplifies in it the history of the human race.[11] In Barth's thinking the awakening to faith on the part of men signifies an acknowledgment of Christ's salvation as over against a realization or fulfillment of this salvation.

In order to do justice to every facet of biblical faith, we must hold that salvation is not only an event in the past but also an event in the present. Those who have died with Christ at Calvary are the same as those who live with Him now in the power of His resurrection. Our death in Christ at Calvary is a reality only for faith. That is to say, our death on Calvary is

[9] The objectivism of Barth can be seen in the following statements: "Even before he becomes a Christian he is in continuity with God in Christ, but he has not yet discovered it. He realizes it only when he begins to believe. . . . The distinction is not between redeemed and nonredeemed, but between those who realize it and those who do not." John Godsey, ed., *Karl Barth's Table Talk* (Edinburgh: Oliver & Boyd, 1963), pp. 15, 87.

[10] Morrison writes: "If *Christ's conquest* does not come about in men, it does not come about at all! For this reason, the Word became flesh, and the Church was ordained to preach the gospel among men. The Church was no mere 'information service' reporting changes in the cosmic organization, but its word was God's power for salvation." *The Powers That Be* (Naperville, Ill.: Alec R. Allenson, Inc., 1960), p. 126.

[11] See explanatory note 12.

organically related to our life in the Spirit. Our salvation is rooted and grounded in the events of sacred history mirrored in the Bible and culminating at Calvary, but these roots will have little reality or meaning for us apart from the fruits of a life of obedience under the cross.

This is not to imply that the cross and resurrection of Christ are realities only for faith. Against Bultmann and Ebeling we maintain that the cross and resurrection have an inherent significance of their own, independent of faith. We also insist that the resurrection is a datable historical event although, unlike the crucifixion, it is not accessible to scientific verification. The resurrection was manifest only to the community of faith (Acts 10:40, 41). At the same time we hold that something objective happened at Calvary and the empty tomb which is beneficial to the whole world. The nature of this benefit is that hell and death have been vanquished, the decisive battle has been won against the powers of darkness. There is now a real possibility for liberation for all men. But this liberation does not become a practical or concrete reality in our lives apart from repentance and faith.

IV

Bearing the Cross

The last chapter concerned the objective basis and past dimension of our salvation. Now we shall discuss the present pole of our salvation — the Christian life. Just as the death on the cross is the past dimension of salvation, so the bearing of the cross by believers is the present pole. The life and death of Jesus Christ are the foundation of our salvation; a life of faith and love on the part of His disciples signifies the realization of salvation in ongoing history.

To be sure, it is possible to speak of Jesus Christ Himself as being both the objective and subjective poles of salvation. Since Christ is our Representative, He includes within His own life-history the history of the chosen or elect community. Again, Christ is the "new man" within every believer. The Christian life is one that is never separated from Him. A life under the cross is a life grounded in and molded by the indwelling Christ. That is to say, we are saved not only by Christ for us (*Christus pro nobis*) but also by Christ in us (*Christus in nobis*). The same apostle who testified that "God was in Christ reconciling the world to himself" (II Cor. 5:19) could also proclaim: "Christ in you, the hope of glory" (Col. 1:27).

Karl Barth has said at one place: "To *be* apprehended is enough. It requires no correlative on my side, and can have none."[1] Insofar as the election of Christ excludes any merit

1 Karl Barth, *The Epistle to the Philippians* (Richmond, Virginia: John Knox Press, 1962), p. 108. In the same commentary Barth quotes Horn with approval: " 'Faith is not mine but God's.' " But this can be interpreted in such a way as to reduce man to a puppet or automaton.

or claim that we can bring from our side, this is a true statement. But as it stands it easily lends itself to misinterpretation. Indeed, in the framework of Barthian theology it reinforces an objectivistic as over against a paradoxical way of thinking. It is true that we are elected by virtue of the mercy of God and not because of deeds done by us in righteousness (Tit. 3:5). Yet if this election is to benefit us we must believe in it. If the death of Christ is to avail for our salvation, we must participate in this death. Paul states that although we might be heirs of the kingdom, we are no better than slaves if we fail to claim our inheritance (Gal. 4:1, 8, 9).

The New Testament underscores the close relation between God's reconciling work in Christ and the obedience of faith. This relationship is certainly witnessed to in John 3:16, which Luther called "the gospel in miniature": "For God so loved the world that he gave his only Son, that whoever believes in him should not perish but have eternal life." John goes on to point out that God sent His Son into the world to save the world but that only those who accept Christ escape condemnation (3:17, 18). The indissoluble connection between faith and obedience is given in verse 36 of the same chapter: "He who believes in the Son has eternal life; he who does not obey the Son shall not see life, but the wrath of God rests upon him." A similar note is to be found in the twelfth chapter of John: "I have come as light into the world, that whoever believes in me may not remain in darkness. If any one hears my sayings and does not keep them . . . the word that I have spoken will be his judge on the last day" (46-48).

Paul writes concerning the gospel: ". . . it is the power of God for salvation to every one who has faith" (Rom. 1:16). And again: "For man believes with his heart and so is justified, and he confesses with his lips and so is saved" (Rom. 10:10). In his letter to the Colossians Paul declares: "And you, who once were estranged and hostile in mind . . . he has now reconciled in his body of flesh by his death . . . provided that you continue in the faith" (Col. 1:21-23; cf. Rom. 11:22). Peter proclaims: "To him all the prophets bear witness that every one who believes in him receives forgiveness of sins through his name" (Acts 10:43). The Epistle to the Hebrews states that Christ "being made perfect . . . became the source of eternal salvation to all who obey him" (Heb. 5:9). The same epistle testifies that God's word or promise can truly help us only if it meets with faith (4:2).

The interdependence of the historical atonement and the Christian life of faith is a note that is sounded repeatedly in the history of Christian theology. It is not our purpose to enumerate the views of numerous theologians on this subject, but it can be shown that the fathers of both Roman Catholicism and Protestantism regarded the relationship of the cross to Christian faith and discipleship as supremely important. Thomas Aquinas has written: "When a sufficient satisfaction has been rendered, liability to punishment is removed . . . but the satisfaction of Christ takes effect in us only in so far as we become one body with Him as members with their head. And the members ought to be conformed to the head."[2] Calvin, despite his heavy emphasis on the objectivity of the work of Christ, could nevertheless affirm: ". . . as long as Christ remains outside of us, and we are separated from him, all that he has suffered and done for the salvation of the human race remains useless and of no value for us. Therefore, to share with us what he has received from the Father, he had to become ours and to dwell within us."[3] And again: ". . . free adoption, in which our salvation consists, is inseparable from this other decree, viz., that He had appointed us to bear the cross. No one can be an heir of heaven who has not first been conformed to the only begotten Son of God."[4] In Luther's view personal appropriation of the sacrifice of Christ is indispensable for our salvation: "For though Christ had been given and crucified for us a thousand times all were profitless if the Word of God came not to administer it and to bestow it upon me and to say, this is for

[2] Thomas Aquinas, *Summa Theologica* (Paris: P. Lethielleux, 1888), Vol. IX, Part III, xlix, Art. iii, body and reply 3, p. 296.

[3] John Calvin, *Institutes of the Christian Religion*, III, 1, 1, p. 537.

[4] John Calvin, *The Epistles of Paul the Apostle to the Romans and to the Thessalonians*, eds. David and Thomas Torrance, trans. R. MacKenzie (Grand Rapids: Wm. B. Eerdmans, 1961), p. 181.

thee."[5] Of the foregoing statements only that of Thomas
Aquinas reflects the truth that Christ accomplished much for
the human race independent of the faith and obedience of believers. But all of these men remind us that the work of Christ
does not make our salvation effectual unless Christ is united
with us in the relationship of faith.

Salvation signifies the conjunction of the moment of the incarnation and the moment of decision. But the moment of
decision or the decision of faith must be understood not simply
as one decision but as a life of decision. The experience of salvation is not merely one specific experience in the life of the
Christian; rather, it consists in an abiding with Christ that is
strengthened and deepened throughout life. Faith entails not
simply the acceptance of Christ but daily repentance and obedience. In Spener's words: ". . . it is by no means enough to
have knowledge of the Christian faith, for Christianity consists
rather of practice."[6] It is not a single experience of conversion
but a life of conversion that is decisive for our salvation.

The subjective pole of salvation is therefore not simply the
experience of the cross but the bearing of the cross. It is not
only believing in the cross but persevering under the cross. It
is *walking* in the light as well as having the light. It is *doing*
the truth as well as hearing the truth (Is. 56:1; Jn. 3:21; Lk.
8:15; Jas. 1:22). Faith and obedience go together, although,
contrary to Bultmann, they are not identical.[7] Faith — a saving
knowledge of Christ — is the root of our salvation; obedience is
the fruit and flower. Before one can act according to the truth,
one must be in the truth (Lk. 6:43-45). Yet there is no being
without acting, just as there is no acting without being.

We are saved *de jure* by the sacrifice of Christ on Calvary.
But we are saved *de facto* by a life of repentance and obedience.
The atoning blood of Christ was sufficient for our salvation, but
we must be sprinkled with this blood (I Pet. 1:2) if it is to be
effectual for our salvation. Moreover, we must be prepared to

[5] Martin Luther, *D. Martin Luther's Werke,* 18 Band (Weimar: Hermann
Boehlaus Nachfolger, 1908), pp. 202, 203.

[6] Philip J. Spener, *Pia Desideria* (Philadelphia: Fortress Press, 1965),
p. 95.

[7] See explanatory note 13.

resist even unto blood (Heb. 12:4), if the cross is to maintain its efficacy. Richard Baxter underlined very forcefully the necessity for the application of the atoning blood of the cross: "It is not a Saviour offered, but received also, that must save: it is not the blood of Christ shed only, but applied also, that must fully deliver; nor is it applied to the justification or salvation of a sleepy soul. . . ."[8]

The Bible teaches that if God's kingdom is to triumph it is not only Christ who must die; but we must die with Him, so that we can live with Him. We must put off the old nature and put on the new. To put on the "new man" or Christ means to take upon oneself the cross. It means to accept the yoke of Christ by taking upon oneself the tribulations and sacrifices that are inherent in being a Christian. If we refuse the cross we can no longer be counted members of His body. As Jesus said: "Whoever does not bear his own cross and come after me, cannot be my disciple" (Lk. 14:27).

Our cross is a mode of suffering and service associated with the new nature. It is a mode of suffering that is especially fitted to one's own existential condition and therefore will be different for every Christian. It might be regarded as the particular road that the child of God is called to walk in order to fulfill his vocation as a suffering servant. Our cross includes the many little crosses which accompany us on this pilgrimage. Kierkegaard rightly discerned that the cross of the Christian is a voluntary as over against an involuntary suffering.

Our new nature springs from Jesus Christ and our suffering is similar to His. Paul could speak of carrying in our bodies the death of Jesus Christ (II Cor. 4:10). Calvin wrote, ". . . in all our miseries we are partakers of Christ's Cross if we are His members."[9] But our suffering is not identical with the suffering of Christ. Like Christ the Christian suffers for others, but not by any means to the same extent. To be sure, Jesus said that we shall drink of the same cup from which He drank (Mk. 10:39).

---

[8] Richard Baxter, *The Saints' Everlasting Rest,* abridged with intro. by John T. Wilkinson (London: Epworth Wilkinson Press, 1962), p. 35.

[9] John Calvin, *Commentaries on the Epistles of Paul the Apostle to the Philippians, Colossians & Thessalonians,* trans. John Pringle (Edinburgh: Calvin Translation Society, 1851), p. 99.

But we shall not drink of this bitter cup of suffering in the same way nor to the same degree.

Our suffering, insofar as it is suffering for the faith, corresponds to the suffering of Christ. This correspondence is made possible by our participation in His life and death. But there is no one-to-one identity between our tribulations and the passion of Christ. We are members of His mystical body, but we are not second Christs. Christ alone is the head of the body. His cross alone atones for the sins of the world.

At this point we might ask ourselves, What is the relation between the receiving and the bearing of the cross? The cross must first be placed upon us before we can carry it. Yet we do not receive it unless we strive to take up the cross. The act of receiving the cross is passive and is equivalent to the new birth. To receive the cross is to be engrafted into Christ. It is to be baptized into His death. It is to be born into the church through His Spirit.

Taking up the cross and bearing the cross refer to the active side of the life of faith. The first is a completed act, the second a continuing act. Yet we are told that we must take up the cross daily (Lk. 9:23); that is to say, we must constantly reaffirm our first decision. It must be recognized that the cross is never our possession. It must be given to us; we hold it only through the Holy Spirit. To take up the cross is equivalent to repentance. Bearing the cross signifies discipleship and service (Lk. 14:27). Taking up the cross means putting on Christ; bearing the cross means walking with Christ.

The act of receiving and taking up the cross is symbolized by the sacrament of baptism. Specific modes of service and cross-bearing are dramatized by such sacramental rites as confirmation, matrimony, and ordination. The sacrament of baptism saves only when related to the decision of faith. That is to say, there is no receiving of the cross apart from the bearing of the cross. There is no genuine election apart from decision. This is why we must affirm that one is incorporated into the church, the mystical body of Christ, not by baptism alone but by baptism and faith (Mk. 16:16; Col. 2:12).

The paradox is that those who receive the cross are precisely those who bear the cross. The paradox in this context refers to a present event. This is the paradox of election and decision, grace and faithful obedience. Grace is given through the Word and the sacraments; but it is incumbent upon us to lay hold of this grace. The indicative and the imperative are combined in the present event of salvation (Bultmann). Paul expresses this paradox very cogently in the following words: ". . . work out your own salvation with fear and trembling; for God is at work in you, both to will and to work for his good pleasure" (Phil. 2:12, 13).

The act of receiving and taking up the cross is a once-for-all event. One can enter the kingdom only in one moment of time. We do not grow into the kingdom; we are reborn into the kingdom. Yet in another sense the act of taking up the cross must be done ever again. The reason is that we cannot make a perfect decision or commitment. Only Christ has made this kind of decision. It can be said that we die *in* Christ once for all insofar as He dies once for all as our Representative (II Cor. 5:14). But we must die *with* Christ daily insofar as our decision for Christ forever remains imperfect and ambiguous. Christ's decision for us, the sign and seal of which is baptism, is final and irrevocable; this is why we can be baptized only once. But we have yet to appropriate all of the fruits of our death in Christ. The full realization of our crucifixion with Christ is still to take place. Yet the paradoxical truth is that we have not died in Christ on Calvary unless we die with Christ in our daily experience. We cannot lay claim to having been baptized with Christ in the experience of faith unless we manifest this death in our ongoing lives.

The mystery of our salvation is certainly set forth in the fact that Christians also are called upon to take up the cross and follow Christ. The cross is given by Christ; it is not a cross of our own choosing. Yet although the cross is laid upon us, it has not yet been fully appropriated by us. This is why Paul urges Christians to put on the new man (Rom. 13:14; Eph. 4:22-24; Col. 3:12-14; I Thes. 5:8). Even Christians are exhorted to repent (Rev. 3:3) and to be converted (Lk. 22:32). Luther pointed to the need to take up the cross continually: "When our

Lord and Master, Jesus Christ, said 'Repent,' He called for the entire life of believers to be one of penitence."[10]

We enter the church through repentance, and we remain in the church through repentance. Even the converted therefore must be told to seek deeper regeneration and renewal (cf. Ps. 51:10-12). The new birth is in one sense a specific event in the past, but in another sense it is a continuous process insofar as the fruits of our baptism into Christ have yet to be fully appropriated. It is significant that in I Peter 1:3, 23 the new birth is described in terms of the Greek perfect tense, thus indicating that the action of the verb continues into the present. Regeneration cannot be separated from the other facets of salvation, particularly perseverance in bearing the cross. If we do not bear fruit, we are told that we shall lose our new nature (Jn. 15: 5, 6).

The relation between receiving and bearing the cross is analogous to that between grace and faith on the one hand and faith and love on the other. We receive the cross by grace through faith; we bear the cross in faithfulness and love.

Faith signifies both passive reception and active decision. Faith is passive insofar as we contribute nothing from within ourselves; but it is active in that we are compelled to respond to and follow Christ. The passive side of faith is being known by God and thereby being awakened to His presence. It is a knowledge grounded in the experience of the new birth. Faith in this sense is participation in Christ by receiving. It signifies a surrender to the Spirit of God. It can be viewed as an experience of being grasped and possessed by the Holy Spirit. The active side of faith is acceptance and trust.[11] It also involves and leads into obedience. A full definition of faith understands it as a commitment of the whole man to the living Christ, a commitment that entails knowledge, trust, and obedience. But the knowledge is prior to the trust and obedience.

The obedience that is involved in faith is obedience not to the law as such but to Christ. Faith is not to be associated with

[10] Bertram Lee Woolf, *Reformation Writings of Martin Luther* (London: Lutterworth Press, 1952) , p. 32.
[11] See explanatory note 14.

legalism or rigorism, but rather with evangelical obedience. This obedience must not be confused with toil in the sense of drudgery (Lk. 5:5-7; 12:27). It is essentially the loving obedience of free men. Such obedience may very well involve heroic striving (Col. 1:29; I Tim. 4:10), which springs from love, not from guilt or neurotic compulsion. The moral law remains the general norm for evangelical obedience; but the indwelling Christ is the power which enables us to fulfill our obligations under the cross. Faith as obedience is taking up the cross and bearing it in love and gratefulness.

Prayer is certainly a prime fruit of faith. Prayer is also a necessary concomitant (if not an integral part) of cross-bearing. Calvin was convinced that ". . . no one can give himself cheerfully to prayer until he has been softened by the cross and thoroughly subdued."[12] Prayer is related to both the passive and active sides of faith: it is waiting upon God in silence and responding to Him in adoration and supplication. Prayer entails not only receiving but also seeking. Indeed, only those who seek to pray are enabled to pray. Just as we can contribute to the advancement of God's kingdom through our cross, so we can contribute to God's glory through our prayer, in that it is inseparably bound up with our cross. Certainly one of the highest forms of prayer is humble supplication, for such prayer reveals and demonstrates our absolute dependence upon God.

Luther compares the relationship of love (*agape*) to faith with that of heat to light. Love accompanies faith in that it immediately springs out of faith. Calvin calls faith the doorway to love. Love might be regarded as the subjective mode of sanctification, just as faith is the subjective mode of justification. Love restores us to the image of God; faith restores us to the favor of God (Wesley). Faith is the human response to God's justifying sentence; love is the human response to God's direction (Barth). Love is directed not only to man but also to God.

We here take issue with Anders Nygren, who in his book *Agape and Eros* contends that true love is only received from God and not given to God. He pictures man as a funnel through

---

12 John Calvin, *Commentary on the Book of Psalms*, trans. James Anderson, Vol. I (Edinburgh: Calvin Translation Society, 1845), p. 495.

which the love of God, *agape,* is poured out to the world. Man is conceived of as an instrument of *agape,* but his own love, *eros,* always stands in opposition to *agape.* It must be recognized that Nygren seeks to separate *agape* and *eros* only in the ideological sense. The object of his attack is not *eros* as actual human love but *eros* as an idea or basic attitude. Yet he fails to relate *agape* and human love in any meaningful or positive way. For Nygren human love is never transformed by *agape* so that it might mirror and witness to the redemption of Christ. Rather, it is either negated or deflected from sinful ends.

In our view love as *agape* certainly comes from God, but it must be exercised by man. It does not overthrow human or natural love but rather transforms and purifies this love. Inasmuch as it is exercised by man, it refers to the active side of man's service to God and his fellow man. We would agree with C. S. Lewis, who holds that the appreciative love of God is the highest kind of love.[13]

The works of love, or faithful works, are the goal and flower of faith. These works are to be distinguished from the works of the law, which are grounded in the desire to make ourselves worthy in the sight of God. We might say that holiness is the fruit of love, just as perseverance is the fruit of faith. Works are the burning, but faith is the fire (Luther). Unless the grace of God is fulfilled in faith and love it is of no avail for man's salvation. Paul made this very clear when he said: "Note . . . God's kindness to you, provided you continue in his kindness; otherwise you too will be cut off" (Rom. 11:22; cf. I Cor. 15:2).

Taking up the cross is an act of faith; bearing the cross is a fruit of faith. Bearing the cross is at the same time the heart and core of love. Bearing the cross signifies both incarnate love and concrete faith. It represents faith and love in action. Life under the cross is a life characterized by faithfulness and long-suffering. It is a life of humble discipleship and loving service. The consummation of such a life is none other than the crown of salvation. As the apostle wrote: "Be faithful unto death, and I will give you the crown of life" (Rev. 2:10).

[13] See C. S. Lewis, *The Four Loves* (New York: Harcourt, Brace & World, Inc., 1960).

Bearing the cross means to suffer *in* Christ and *for* Christ. This suffering must not be confused with the afflictions which come to man because of his misdeeds. Nor is bearing the cross necessarily the same as bearing misfortune. Since there is a reason for every affliction, there is no such thing as "misfortune." We will either suffer divine retribution for our sins or else we will suffer rejection by the world for the sake of Christ. We will suffer either the pangs of guilt and despair or the anguish of vicarious love. The yoke of Christ is something other than the yoke of sin (I Pet. 4:14-16). The suffering of the cross refers not to the sorrows of this world (II Cor. 7:10) but to the tribulations of faith. To be sure, any kind of affliction can become a "tribulation of faith" once it is offered up to God as a sacrifice for the good of others.[14] Tribulations are given to us in order to test and purify us and thereby to deepen our union with the crucified and risen Christ. Such tribulations are to be regarded not as penalties for sin but rather as disciplines that enable us to overcome sin. In evangelical theology the Christian no longer suffers penalties for sin, since Christ has taken away all penalties by His atoning death on the cross.

This brings us to the question of whether there is suffering that should be viewed as completely senseless, which can be meaningfully related to neither sin nor salvation. There is, of course, much suffering that is senseless from a purely human standpoint, and yet we must remember that although it may not make sense to man it does have meaning and purpose in the eyes of God. Even the man who was born blind was permitted to suffer so that God might be glorified in Christ (Jn. 9:1-3). Even though the blind man lacked faith at the time, his suffering was for the sake of Christ and the glory of God. Perhaps one can also say that he suffered affliction and rejection because of his future faith.

In that our cross mirrors the cross of Christ and turns us ever again to His cross, it has redemptive significance not only for us but for the world. The suffering of faith by revealing and proclaiming the atoning sacrifice of Christ contributes to the efficacy and fruitfulness of this sacrifice. Bearing the cross can therefore

14 See explanatory note 15.

be regarded in one sense as redemptive suffering, since it attests and communicates the redemption of Jesus Christ (cf. II Cor. 1:5, 6; 4:12; 7:10; II Tim. 2:10). Calvin averred: " . . . Paul not only exhorts us to exhibit an example of Christ's death but declares that there inheres in it an efficacy which ought to be manifest in all Christians, unless they intend to render his death useless and unfruitful."[15]

Bearing the cross has been associated in the history of the church with mortification and self-denial (cf. Mt. 16:24). It can be said to signify self-denial after the pattern of Christ. It essentially means the imitation of Christ (*imitatio Christi*). As the imitation of Christ, bearing the cross has four basic facets or meanings.

First of all, it means bearing the trials of temptation. It entails enduring and resisting the onslaught of evil. It means wrestling with and overcoming sinful desire, just as Christ wrestled with and conquered demonic temptation. Christ, to be sure, was forever triumphant in His battles with sin and darkness, whereas His disciples fall ever again. Just as Christ denied Himself in order to fulfill His vocation, so we should deny ourselves for the sake of our fulfillment and salvation. In the decision of faith the burden of guilt and sin was lifted from us, but a saddened awareness remains of the dying but persistent desire to return to our wretched past. The Christian as a "new man" has been set free from the compulsion to sin and its corollary the anxiety of guilt. But now he is beset by temptations more acute and virulent than those experienced by hardened sinners, since the devil seeks to drag down the children of light. The Christian will have sorrow over his aberrant desire and his frequent yielding to temptation, but this sorrow is mitigated by the assurance that his sins are forgiven and covered by Christ. This assurance becomes a reality for man in the act of repentance.

The cross that is placed upon the Christian is not a new burden but rather a shield which enables him to withstand and overcome the temptation to sin. He suffers no longer as a lost, tormented sinner but as a repentant and conquering saint. In-

15 John Calvin, *Institutes of the Christian Religion*, II, 16, 7, p. 512.

sofar as temptation and sin continue to intrude into the life of the Christian, he will forever be threatened by the very kind of burden which was taken away by Christ at Calvary. But this burden will not again become an integral part of his existence unless he refuses to repent and thereby falls away from faith itself. The Christian will always be conscious of his susceptibility to temptation. He will have an acute awareness of his sin and weakness (cf. Ps. 51:3); this is the one tribulation that is indispensable to the life of faith. But again we must contend that this is an awareness of that which has been overcome through the atoning death of Christ and which is being overcome anew through the power of His Spirit.

Second, bearing the cross means bearing the burdens of others, thereby fulfilling the law of Christ (Gal. 6:2). As Christ came to serve and minister unto men, so we should seek to do the same, for the disciple is not above his master (Mt. 10:24). The disciple of Christ will embrace a vocation of loving sacrificial service and intercessory prayer. He will deny himself for the sake of the world for which Christ died. The service to others includes not only self-giving love or charity (*caritas*) but also social action wherever necessary. Insofar as we unite our cross-bearing with the suffering of Christ, our cross is given a role in the work of redemption. To suffer vicariously for others means to share Christ's passion and concern for the downhearted and the broken in spirit. This burden must not be confused with the burden of our sin that was cast off in the decision of faith. Rather, it refers to a loving identification with the burdens of our neighbor. This burden has been rightly called the yoke of righteousness or the yoke of Christ. Moreover, Christ tells us that His yoke is easy and His burden is light (Mt. 11:30).

A third basic meaning of bearing the cross is upholding and proclaiming the cross of faith. Just as Jesus heralded the kingdom message, so we too must uphold and bear witness to this message in our words and actions. Such fidelity to the truth of faith, which speaks to every area of life, will invariably bring us into conflict with the principalities and powers of the world. Jesus was confronted by the powers of darkness in the wilderness and many other times in His ministry, but He refused to swerve from His sacred mission. To bear the cross consequently means to be a soldier of the cross under the banner of the gospel. It involves putting on the armor of light and taking up "the sword of the Spirit, which is the word of God" (Rom. 13:12; Eph. 6:17). It means to suffer persecution and rejection by the world (Lk. 21:16, 17; Heb. 13:13; II Tim. 3:12). This kind of cross-bearing signifies self-denial for the Word. It entails humble supplication and incarnate or concrete witnessing.

Fourth, bearing the cross includes contemplation of the cross of Christ. Certainly Jesus meditated on His approaching death in Gethsemane and indeed throughout His entire ministry. Bearing the cross in this sense means to hold up His cross before oneself and meditate upon the passion of Christ. It involves reflection upon and confession of our sins as the cause of Christ's death. This is a suffering born out of the recollection of Christ's crucifixion and issuing in contrition and renewed dedication. Just as Jesus renounced the works of the devil and was obedient to the point of death, so we too must renounce these works and our involvement in them and seek to be like Jesus in His death (Phil. 3:10). This is self-denial for the sake of one's own edification and consolation. This kind of cross-bearing has often been more prevalent in Catholic mysticism than in Reformation thought. Yet meditation on the sufferings of Christ can also be found in the Reformers, including Luther.[16] The paradox is that we come to a true knowledge of ourselves by focusing our attention on the suffering love of Christ as manifested in His death.

All the facets of our self-denial or cross-bearing that have been discussed are of course interrelated. When we identify ourselves with the sufferings of others we are denying ourselves not only for the sake of the world but also for the glory of Christ and for our own salvation. But denial for the sake of others seems to be especially prominent in this form of cross-bearing. A case can be made for the presence of all forms of self-denial

[16] See Adolf Köberle, *The Quest for Holiness*, trans. from the Third German Edition by John Mattes (Minneapolis: Augsburg Publishing House, 1938), pp. 159, 160.

in the other types of cross-bearing. It also must be said that
warfare with the demonic powers is involved in every form of
bearing the cross.

Some theologians today sharply criticize the concept of the
imitation of Christ.[17] These men maintain that we should follow the living Christ. But does not the living Christ point us
to His own incarnate life as our example and guide? The historic Jesus is certainly the norm for obedience to the Christ of
faith. Paul wrote that he bore on his body the marks of Jesus
(Gal. 6:17). Moreover, he calls upon Christians to follow his
example as he follows the example of Christ (I Cor. 4:16; 11:1;
cf. Phil. 3:17). In Paul's mind the imitation of Christ does not
necessarily consist in copying Christ in externals; rather, it is
being conformed to His image in any situation in which we
find ourselves (cf. I Cor. 7:17-24).

Bearing the cross is integrally related to the humiliation, passion, and death of Christ. It signifies a sharing or participation
in the priestly work of Christ. It consists not only in an imitation of the sufferings of Christ but also in a participation in
these sufferings (I Pet. 4:13; II Cor. 1:5; Phil. 3:10). It involves
a sharing in the agony of Christ, not only in His agonizing death
on the cross but also in His present passion. Bearing the cross
signifies a mystical identification with the sufferings of Christ,
but only in the sense of being in direct contact with Christ
through His Spirit. As has already been intimated, this by no
means implies that our sufferings are on the same level as His.

Bearing the cross is also related to the victory and exaltation
of Christ. That is to say, it signifies a sharing in the kingly
work of Christ. It is a means by which we participate in His
resurrection and ascension. Just as the death on the cross prepared the way for the resurrection from the grave, so the bearing of the cross is the pre-condition for the new life in Christ.
Bearing the cross gives us strength to live the new life. Con-
versely, we are able to live the new life by bearing the cross.

17 For example, see Regin Prenter, *Spiritus Creator*, trans. John M. Jen-
son (Philadelphia: Muhlenburg Press, 1953), pp. 10, 11, 28, 50f., 210f., 253.
Karl Barth and Emil Brunner have also raised questions concerning the imitation of Christ.

We must ask ourselves what relation the bearing of the cross has to the means of grace. For the Roman Catholic Church the means of grace are primarily the sacraments; preaching, service, and instruction are secondary instruments of the Spirit of God. The Reformers regarded the preaching of the Word as the decisive channel of redemption. In the Roman Catholic view the Christian life is primarily not a means of bringing grace to our neighbor but rather a means of accumulating and retaining grace for ourselves. For the Protestant Reformers the Christian life is a sign or fruit of grace rather than a means of grace.

Our position is that there are both objective and subjective means of grace. We concur in the view that the objective means include the Word and the sacraments. But the Christian life can also be regarded as an objective means of grace, in that the Spirit of God reaches out to men through the testimony and life of the children of God. Certainly an act of kindness can be viewed as a means of conversion (I Pet. 2:12; 3:1, 2). Even Luther recognized this: "Thus also God converts those whom he converts by showing them his goodness. And this is the only way to convert anyone: to show him love and kindness."[18] Christ acts not only *for* us and *in* us but also *through* us. This is to say that we participate in the prophetic office of Christ as well. The witness of our life (which includes our words) is a means of revelation to a world blinded by ignorance and sin.

Certainly intercessory prayer is one of the most potent means of grace and can contribute much to the welfare and liberation of man. Bonhoeffer recognized the power of prayer when he affirmed: "Intercession, like every other form of prayer, cannot compel God, but if he himself gives the final sanction then a man can ransom his brother, by virtue of the church."[19] Much is said today of mass evangelism and visitation evangelism, but very little of prayer evangelism. Indeed, prayer evangelism

[18] Martin Luther, *Luther: Lectures on Romans,* ed. and trans. Wm. Pauck (Philadelphia: Westminster Press, 1961), p. 356.
[19] Dietrich Bonhoeffer, *Sanctorum Communio,* trans. R. Gregor Smith (London: Collins, 1963), p. 133.

might be regarded as the neglected factor in the life of the modern church.

The Christian life must also be seen as the subjective means of grace. The Word is given not only from faith but also to faith (Rom. 1:17). The Word of God can be neither rightly perceived nor fully assimilated apart from seeking and believing. Nor can it be retained by those to whom it is given apart from their prayer, obedience, and service. This dimension or facet of the means of grace has been woefully neglected in the circles of orthodoxy (both Catholic and Protestant). Word and life belong together. Our witness should be one of word and deed (Rom. 15:18), and our commitment should also involve thought, word, and act. Dogmatics must never be separated from ethics: the *theologia dogmatica* must be combined with the *theologia practica*. Evangelism must be held in creative tension with social action. The proclaimed word must be united with the silent word of ministering love.

Not only do word and life belong together, but the word and the world must be conjoined. This is an emphasis that is receiving much attention in contemporary theology. The truth in this emphasis is that the message of faith must be applied and related to the specific problems of the world. Theology apart from sociology is no more alive than sociology apart from theology. Yet we must guard against deriving the truth-content of the faith from the world's interpretation of itself.

Our objection to Tillich's method of correlation is that he tends to let the questions of the culture prescribe how the answer of the faith is to be formulated and even understood. Cultural philosophy would seem to determine not only the language but also the concepts of faith in Tillich's theology. The mission of the church is not to build upon the creative self-interpretation of the culture, but rather to challenge and overthrow this self-interpretation. We should seek to bring our hearers to the point where they will ask the questions of faith, since only these questions are properly answered by the message of faith.

In considering the Christian life in the world we must ponder the question whether bearing the cross totally excludes wielding the sword. Certainly taking up the sword is precluded in defense of the kingdom of God, since this kingdom is defended only by the Word (cf. Mt. 26:52). Yet does discipleship under the cross mean that we are helpless to defend our loved ones against attack? Does such discipleship predicate the abdication of our responsibilities in the secular realm, namely, the maintaining of justice and order, which may necessitate the use of force? The Anabaptists generally held that the bearing of the cross requires an absolute pacifism, and here we would part company with them (despite our common concern for Christian discipleship). We are members both of a divinely instituted church and of the secular state, and we owe duties to each (Rom. 13:1-7). But church and state are not to be correlated with the kingdoms of light and darkness respectively (which was the besetting temptation of Lutheran pietism). Both the church and the secular realm participate in the kingdom of light and both are threatened by the kingdom of darkness. The church must be viewed as a leaven within the state reminding the state that it too exists under the lordship and kingship of Christ. Bearing the cross of course does not predicate blind obedience to the state and may certainly involve disloyalty when the state transgresses the divinely given norms of justice.

The peril of nuclear war has caused many Christians to reappraise their relationship to the state and has impressed upon them the truth that the state is to be given only a relative loyalty. Indeed, it is a real question whether a Christian can participate in modern nuclear warfare, since weapons of mass extermination that would maim and torture and kill not only an attacking army but also millions not directly involved in the struggle are certainly out of bounds for those who seek to be children of light. Such weapons are also capable of maiming millions yet unborn, as well as disfiguring nature itself. Any war in which these weapons are used can no longer be considered a "just war" in any sense of this word. Many theologians today, among them Karl Barth and Arthur Cochrane, rightly hold that bearing the cross in the contemporary situation necessarily entails nuclear pacifism.

Another question in this connection is whether bearing the

cross precludes bearing the cares of family life and property. The Roman Catholic position is that the highest form of discipleship involves the renouncing of family and property for the purpose of exclusive service to Christ. Catholic theologians point to the rich young ruler who was told by Jesus to sell all if he would be perfect (Mk. 10:17-22). They interpret this command of Jesus as a "counsel of perfection," which is addressed to those valiant souls who would seek a more direct or surer path to heaven. An evangelical would hold that this command must be interpreted contextually, not as a general requirement for Christians nor even one that is binding on those who would be true or full disciples. Rather, it is a command that is obligatory for the rich man and others who find their riches to be a stumbling block or barrier in the service of the kingdom.

The counsel to celibacy as given in Matthew 19:10-12 must also not be regarded as referring to a more perfect or higher way to salvation. This counsel can be accepted by those who discern in celibacy a more practical way of serving Christ in the situation in which they find themselves. There is certainly a place for the witness of those who espouse poverty and celibacy for the sake of Christian mission, and Protestantism has on the whole neglected this way of service to its detriment. The present revival of community life in Protestantism is to be welcomed in that it reminds us that discipleship exists not only in the world but also apart from and against the world.[20] Yet those who renounce the world outwardly are not to be regarded as more worthy or holy in the sight of God than those who bear their cross in the midst of home and family. Indeed, marriage and family, when grounded in Christ, can be regarded as particular modes of cross-bearing which certainly serve to strengthen faith and advance the cause of the kingdom.

It is interesting to note that in the tradition of Christian mysticism there is a constant attempt to hold in balance a life of prayer and a life of active service in the world. Such mystics as Meister Eckhart and Teresa of Avila tended to admire

---

20 See Donald G. Bloesch, *Centers of Christian Renewal* (Philadelphia: United Church Press, 1964).

Martha more than Mary, since Martha was given to loving service, which is seen to be the final goal of contemplation (cf.
Lk. 10:38-42). Our view is that we need both Marthas and
Marys. Perhaps in our American culture with its emphasis on
busyness and togetherness more attention should be given to
Mary. Yet it must be recognized that every child of God is
called to full-time service in His kingdom, whatever form this
might take.

It was the genius of the Reformation that it heralded the
universal call to discipleship and the potentially sacred character of even menial vocations. The Reformers contended that
all Christians are called to the narrow way of discipleship; we
must all surrender any claim or right to family and possessions.
We must present our very selves as living sacrifices for the sake
of the kingdom. In the words of Luther's hymn "A Mighty Fortress": "Let goods and kindred go, / This mortal life also. . . ."
Calvin averred: "Self-denial also implies that we yield up to
God in our hearts all our actual riches and possessions. . . . A
Christian must indeed thus forsake everything he possesses in
order to follow Jesus Christ."[21] Yet it was the position of the
Reformers that the sacrifice that we are called to make is essentially an inward one. Only in some cases does our inward
sacrifice become obvious to the world because of the outward
path which God calls us to follow. In the cases of both Luther
and Calvin their crosses were manifest to the world and their
heroism cannot be denied.[22] The same can be said for Zwingli,
who was slain on the battlefield because of his convictions.[23]
But the Reformers remind us that the cross that Christians
must bear is not necessarily the heroic one of our own choosing
but the often humdrum cross of His appointment. The real
suffering is inward, and outward circumstances may veil rather

[21] Ronald Wallace, *Calvin's Doctrine of the Christian Life* (Grand Rapids:
Wm. B. Eerdmans, 1959), p. 61. Calvin also said in this section: "God may
not will to take these earthly possessions from us but we can continue to
hold them only as we constantly deny them to ourselves and hold them for
the Lord." It must be remembered that Calvin's home actually functioned
as a house of hospitality and that he died in virtual poverty.
[22] See explanatory note 16.
[23] See explanatory note 17.

than reveal our cross, which is known in its full dimensions only by God.

One final question concerns the motivation for bearing the cross. The Protestant Reformers pointed to gratitude or thankfulness as the basic motivation for good works. Roman Catholic theology has placed the emphasis on the desire for salvation. Actually the Bible speaks of many motivations including the will to glorify God, the love of God and neighbor, and the fear of God. Karl Barth has stressed the superiority of love as a compelling motive for Christian service as over against fear. As in so many cases, this is not a question of either-or but of both-and. Certainly Jesus pointed to both the desire for salvation and the fear of God as legitimate motivations for taking up the cross (cf. Mt. 16:24-27; Lk. 12:4, 5). The love of Christ should definitely be a prime factor in moving us to action, but the fear of losing our salvation is not to be discounted. The Anglo-Catholic John Keble was not far from the truth when he concluded one of his hymns with these words: "Save, Lord, by love or fear."[24]

The grace of God is free but not cheap. It cost God His only Son, and it must also cost us our very lives. The sacrifice of God in Christ demands from us a daily sacrifice for the welfare and salvation of others. There is no such thing as "instant salvation" or "instant Christianity." Salvation is not consummated in a moment (although it has its beginning in a moment) ; rather, it is appropriated and actualized through lifelong striving and conflict. It is not any particular experience that saves us but rather bearing the cross in faith and love. It is not any inward vision nor external rite as such but the entire Christian life that is decisive for our salvation. In Roman Catholic theology one finds the view that salvation can be gained or earned.[25] The dominant strand of Neo-Reformation theology contends that salvation can only be acknowledged and proclaimed.[26] Our position is that salvation must be appropriated and realized in a Christian life.

24 John Keble, "When God of Old Came Down From Heaven," *The Methodist Hymnal* (London: Methodist Publishing House, 1954) , p. 106.
25 See explanatory note 18.
26 See explanatory note 19.

V

The Crown of Glory

Our salvation has not only a past and present dimension but
also a future dimension. In addition to holding that we *have
been saved* and that we are now *being saved* we must affirm
that we *shall be saved.* Soteriology leads into and is fulfilled in
eschatology. To be sure, Christ is the author of our salvation,
but He has not yet completed what He began on the cross. He
dwells within us now through His Spirit, but He is coming
again in corporeal form with His angels in order to set up the
kingdom that shall have no end. All things were created through
Christ, and all things will be consummated in Him. The book
of Revelation portrays Christ as "the Alpha and the Omega,
the first and the last, the beginning and the end" (Rev. 22:13).
He is the one "who was and is and is to come" (Rev. 4:8).

Since the consummation of our salvation lies in the future, we
are saved not only by faith but also by hope (Rom. 8:24). As
Brunner says, faith contains hope within itself because faith
knows of the solution without possessing it. Faith looks forward
to the time when the veil of flesh will be taken away and man
will be able to perceive the glory of God directly. Faith is necessary in the interim period, in the time between the resurrection
of Christ and His second advent. But on the last day faith will
be supplanted by sight and the mortal will put on immortality.
On that day the disciple of Christ will be perfected in love
and clothed in glory.

The Christian hope is none other than the crown of glory,
the symbol of final consummation and perfection in Christ.

This is not to say that this-worldly hopes must be discounted or ignored. Because Christ is present with us now in His Word and Spirit, there can be much joy and blessedness in this life. If we make our chief concern His kingdom and His righteousness, the things of this life will be ours as well (Mt. 6:33). At the same time this-worldly hopes are to be regarded as relative and secondary. In Johann Schroeder's words, we are often called to bury the hopes of today and tomorrow so that Jesus Christ, who alone is the priceless treasure, might again have first place in our lives. We can experience much happiness in this life even apart from the direct action of the Spirit because we have been formed in God's image and the world that God created is good. At the same time because of our inveterate sin and hardheartedness, there will never be joy apart from anguish. The peace that can be ours will always be a peace born out of struggle and conflict. The sweetness that we can experience in this life will always be a bitter sweetness. The only crown that we can know in this life is a crown of thorns, a crown that is inseparable from our cross and might be regarded as a sign of the coming crown of glory.

Contemporary theology for the most part has placed the emphasis on some form of realized eschatology as over against futuristic eschatology. This means that the truth that Christ has already come is taken to mean that this is His only coming, that this is none other than the *eschaton* (end) and the *parousia* (appearing). C. H. Dodd holds that God's kingdom is already in operation and that eternal life is a present reality. Bultmann's position differs from the main school of realized eschatology, in that he holds that Christ comes to man ever again in the situation of preaching and hearing. For Bultmann the kingdom is realized anew in the decision of faith.[1] John Robinson identifies the second coming of Christ with the gift of the

---

1 Bultmann's eschatology has been termed "existential" and "realizing," because he holds that the new eon is a reality only for faith. His position differs from that of Dodd in that the kingdom is not believed to be objectively established or realized with Christ's coming, but it must be laid hold of ever again in the decision of faith.

Holy Spirit to the church.[2] Barth contends that the new eon
has already been established by the incarnation of Christ and
that all that remains is for this wonderful fact to be revealed.[3]

There is much truth in these present-day reappraisals of
Christian eschatology. The Fourth Gospel in particular gives
much support to the position that the new age is a present
reality. Yet even in that book the future aspect of our salvation
is not denied; on the contrary, it is explicitly affirmed (cf. Jn.
5:28, 29; 6:44; 12:48). It is true that eternal life begins now,
but life in eternity lies in the future. Now we have an earnest
of our inheritance (Eph. 1:14), but we do not yet possess the
inheritance itself. The New Testament warns against the view
that the resurrection is already behind us (II Tim. 2:18) or
that we are now in the day of the Lord (II Thes. 2:2).

The truth that Christ has already come must not be denied.
The new eon has already been inaugurated by Christ, but the
old eon has not yet passed away. The powers of darkness have
been mortally wounded at the cross, but they have not yet been
totally vanquished. The second advent will usher in something
new, not merely reveal a victory that has taken place in the
past. What remains is not simply for the veil to be taken away
but for the devil to be banished and for death to be annihilated.
We do not look forward to a universal acknowledgment of
God's triumph, thereby ushering in a period of eternal peace;
but rather we await the cataclysmic end of the world by fire
and the creation of a new heaven and a new earth.

What is being said is that one is not fully saved until he has
gained possession of the crown. Believing in the cross is only
a beginning. Yet we have the assurance on the basis of the
promises in Scripture that God will fulfill in His children the
work that He began on the cross. As Paul says, "I am sure that

[2] According to Robinson, what remains is simply for the work of Christ
to run its course. See his *Jesus and His Coming*, 2nd ed. (London: SCM
Press, Ltd., 1962), pp. 160f. Also see his *In the End, God* (London: James
Clarke & Co., Ltd., 1958).

[3] Barth does not deny a second coming, but he holds that this simply
means the revelation of what has already taken place: "Nothing which
will be has not already taken place on Easter Day — included and anticipated in the person of the one man, Jesus Christ." *Church Dogmatics*, III,
2, trans. G. W. Bromiley, *et al.* (Edinburgh: T. & T. Clark, 1960), p. 489.

he who began a good work in you will bring it to completion
at the day of Jesus Christ" (Phil. 1:6). At the same time
God's work is accomplished only through our daily mortification and striving. "But he who endures to the end will be
saved" (Mk. 13:13).

The fact that the coming again of Christ will usher in the
final resurrection of the dead and the last judgment means that
justification has a future aspect. In Denney's words: "The final
sentence of *dikaioi* has not yet been pronounced, and we look
out with eagerness for it."[4] To be sure, we have already been
justified by the sacrificial death of Christ on Calvary. This
justification becomes ours through faith. But on the last day
we shall be judged according to our works (Rom. 2:6f.; II Cor.
5:10). Our works will be accepted so long as we have faith;
indeed, these works are none other than the fruits of our faith.
At the same time justification is not completed until not only
the sinner but also his deeds are justified. This is what Calvin
means when he speaks of a double justification — that of the
sinner and that of the sinner's works.

The Christian life is not a finalized victory but rather a
striving towards victory. It is an unceasing struggle against sin,
death, and the devil. Through faith we are saved from the con-
trolling power of sin, but the presence of sin lingers on in our
lives. Although the Christian is dead to sin (Rom. 6:10, 11),
he can still yield his members to sin (Rom. 6:13). That is to
say, salvation in its fullness is not yet in our grasp.

That faith is a struggle is certainly testified to in Scripture.
The writer of I Timothy says: "Fight the good fight of the faith;
take hold of the eternal life to which you were called when you
made the good confession in the presence of many witnesses"
(I Tim. 6:12; cf. 4:10). Paul writes: "Do you not know that in
a race all the runners compete, but only one receives the prize?
So run that you may obtain it" (I Cor. 9:24). Hebrews urges:
"Strive . . . for the holiness without which no one will see the
Lord" (Heb. 12:14), and again: ". . . let us also lay aside every
weight, and sin which clings so closely, and let us run with per-

[4] James Denney, *The Christian Doctrine of Reconciliation* (London:
James Clarke & Co., Ltd., 1959), p. 116.

severance the race that is set before us" (Heb. 12:1). The need for struggle in the Christian life is nowhere more cogently expressed than by Paul in his letter to the Philippians:

> Not that I have already obtained this or am already perfect; but I press on to make it my own, because Christ Jesus has made me his own. Brethren, I do not consider that I have made it my own; but one thing I do, forgetting what lies behind and straining forward to what lies ahead, I press on toward the goal for the prize of the upward call of God in Christ Jesus (Phil. 3:12-14; cf. 2:12).

The Christian is repeatedly depicted as a soldier of the cross who must clothe himself in the armor of salvation if he is to withstand the onslaughts of the devil (cf. Rom. 13:12; Eph. 6:10f.; II Tim. 2:3, 4). The battle between the church and the powers of darkness is nowhere more graphically described than in Revelation 12. According to Revelation it is only the church militant that will triumph over darkness. It is only the soldier of the cross who will finally gain the crown. Thomas a Kempis reaffirms the Scriptural emphasis on warfare and struggle:

> Always be ready for the battle if you wish for victory; you cannot win the crown of patience without a struggle; if you refuse to suffer you refuse the crown. Therefore, if you desire the crown, fight manfully and endure patiently. Without labor, no rest is won; without battle, there can be no victory.[5]

Our salvation is secure through faith, but it is not guaranteed, since we can fall away from faith. That the child of God can fail to gain his inheritance and forfeit God's grace is amply attested in Scripture (cf. Ezek. 18:24; Gal. 5:4; Heb. 4:6; 6:4-6; I Tim. 1:19; II Pet. 2:20, 21). It is the sons of the kingdom who will be thrown into the outer darkness (Mt. 8:12; 13:41, 42; 24:45f.). Many who are called will finally be rejected (Mt. 22:1-14; 25:1-13). Even Calvin, who emphasized the security of the saints, could nevertheless write:

> Still our redemption would be imperfect if he did not lead us ever onward to the final goal of salvation. Accordingly, the moment we turn away even slightly from him, our salvation,

---

[5] Thomas à Kempis, *The Imitation of Christ*, trans. Leo Sherley-Price (London: Whitefriars Press, 1959), p. 116.

which rests firmly in him, gradually vanishes away. As a result, all those who do not repose in him voluntarily deprive themselves of all grace.[6]

At the same time the Christian can take heart in his battle with the powers of darkness because he has the assurance that the Spirit of Christ dwells within him and enables him to secure the victory. Indeed, the Christian knows that in the last analysis it is the Holy Spirit who wins the victory for us, sometimes even against our own efforts. We are called to press on towards the goal, but from God's perspective we are carried towards this goal by His Spirit. The crown of glory is a gift of God just as our cross is a gift. The Spirit of God completes and crowns our broken efforts and indeed makes these efforts possible.

We can have victory through the Spirit. Therefore our security is in God and not in ourselves. Yet the paradox is that only those who strive have the assurance of the Spirit. Only those who are faithful to Christ are secure in Christ. Only those who work out their salvation have the certainty of salvation.[7] Calvin voiced this paradox in the following way: "He alone is secure who daily strives to advance."[8]

Eternal life is a gift as well as a task. This truth is reflected in Jesus' parables of the kingdom. Jesus likened the kingdom to a pearl of great price, but one must sell everything one has in order to gain possession of this pearl (Mt. 13:45, 46). He also compared it to a treasure in the field, but one must give up all if he would have this treasure (Mt. 13:44). The crown of glory is a free gift of God, but one must overcome self in order to lay hold of it. Richard Baxter reminds us of the necessity for works of faith:

> Let men cry down works while they please, you shall find that these are the conditions of the crown; so that God will not alter the course of justice to give you Rest, before you have laboured; nor the crown of glory till you have overcome.[9]

[6] John Calvin, *Institutes of the Christian Religion*, II, 16, 1, p. 503.

[7] See explanatory note 20.

[8] John Calvin, Comm. II Peter 3:18. *Corpus Reformatorum* LXXXIII (New York: Johnson Reprint Corporation, 1964), p. 480.

[9] Richard Baxter, *The Saints' Everlasting Rest*, abridged ed. (London: Epworth Press, 1962), p. 93.

The Christian life is a race as well as a state of waiting. Salvation is a prize as well as a gift. This prize is the "crown of life" or the "crown of glory." It is a crown or blessing that is "imperishable" or "incorruptible" (I Cor. 9:25). We do not merit this prize, yet it is not given to us apart from good works. We cannot grasp it through our own power, but the Holy Spirit will seize it for us if we persevere in faith and repentance.

This brings us to the precise nature of the crown of salvation. This crown signifies none other than Christian perfection or glorification. Francis of Assisi described it in terms of "perfect joy." Wesley spoke of "perfect love" and "entire sanctification."[10] St. Paul spoke in terms of "perfect holiness" (II Cor. 7:1) and "mature manhood" (Eph. 4:13). Perfection is the goal towards which we are commanded to strive (Mt. 5:48; Heb. 6:1; I Thes. 5:23; II Cor. 7:1), but it is always a goal, never a possession. Still, this goal can be anticipated (Rom. 8:23; Eph. 1:14; I Jn. 2:5; 4:12), but only fragmentarily.

The reason why perfection must be conceived in eschatological terms is that our regeneration is only partial. Calvin maintained that regeneration, though begun in baptism, "does not take place in one moment or in one day or one year."[11] Rather, it is effectuated "through continual and sometimes even slow advances. . . ."[12] The new birth does not mean that our salvation is given to us all at one time but that we begin to receive it. Our conversion does not mean that we are perfected but rather that we are turned towards perfection. Calvin pointed to the necessity of a continuous conversion: "And since this regeneration is never accomplished as long as we are in the prison of this mortal body, it is necessary that the cure of repentance continues until we die."[13]

10 See explanatory note 21.
11 John Calvin, *Institutes*, III, 3, 9, p. 601.
12 *Ibid.* Cf. Luther: ". . . this work of renewal and purification is not completed all at once, but He daily labors with us and purifies us so that we become continuously purer and purer." *Dr. Martin Luther's Sämmtliche Werke*, 8 Band (Erlangen: Verlag von Carl Hender, 1827), p. 175.
13 John Calvin, *Instruction in Faith*, trans. Paul Fuhrmann (Philadelphia: Westminster Press, 1959), p. 43. Calvin's view on regeneration contrasts with that of later Reformed theologians who held that regeneration is consummated in a single moment. See Heinrich Heppe, *Reformed Dogmatics*,

It is not the possession of perfection but the striving after perfection that characterizes the Christian life. We are urged to press on to perfection (Phil. 3:12; Heb. 6:1). In baptism we have been made holy in Christ, but we are called to become holy in all manner of living (I Pet. 1:15). Paul admonishes the faithful to increase and grow and abound in sanctification (Eph. 4:15), in the work of the Lord (I Cor. 15:58; II Cor. 9:8) and in the love of the brethren and of all men (I Thes. 3:12). It must be recognized that in the New Testament a relative or proximate state of perfection is regarded as a possibility for the Christian in this life (cf. Phil. 3:15; Jas. 1:4). At the same time we will always fall short of the ideal of perfect love to which Christ summons us (Mt. 5:48; 22:37) because of sinful desire which lingers in us even after the root of sin has been eradicated.[14] The removal of the blight of sin in the decision of faith might be likened to the extraction of an abscessed tooth. Just as some of the poison that the tooth has emitted remains in the system, so a sinful desire persists even in the man who has been born again. It is this desire or concupiscence that makes us susceptible to temptation (Jas. 1:14). Paul complained: "I can will what is right, but I cannot do it" (Rom. 7:18). Most commentators agree that Paul is referring to his Christian experience in Romans 7. Yet Paul holds that through the grace of Jesus he is able to accomplish that which he could not do through his own efforts (cf. Rom. 8:2-4; Phil. 4:13). Through the work of the Holy Spirit we can attain a certain degree or measure of perfection. We can anticipate and mirror the perfection or sainthood that is in Christ, but we cannot be fully perfect as long as we are in a weakened condition and are thereby vulnerable to the ravages of sin.

The striving for perfection must be understood as the seeking for Christ, who is the ground and embodiment of perfection. Christ is encountered in the decision of faith, but He must be sought for ever again if we are to be perfectly united with Him.

ed. Ernst Bizer (London: George Allen & Unwin, Ltd., 1950), p. 519. The Westminster Confession reflects Calvin's view only at one place; ch. XIII speaks of "the regenerate part (of believers)."
14 See explanatory note 22.

Luther pointed to the necessity for the continual seeking of Christ: "But once found, he wants to be still further sought for and again and again to be found. We find him when we are converted to him from our sins and we seek him as we persevere in this conversion."[15]

The Christian life can be pictured as an ascent to perfection. The Bible speaks not only of the *dove* which symbolizes the descent of the Spirit but also of the *eagle* which represents the ascent of the saint. In the circles of Christian mysticism this ascent has been described in terms of the "Ascent to Mount Carmel" and the "Ascent to Mount Zion." The mystics have also spoken of the "ladder to heaven" which proceeds from the sensate to the spiritual world. Luther attacked the ladder of merit, but he substituted a ladder of faith. Thérèse of Lisieux in her emphasis on free grace speaks of a "lift to heaven."[16]

Christian perfection is not an abstract norm but rather a concrete union with Christ. The call to perfection is a call to surrender and obedience to Christ. We must seek the perfection that is in Him and can be ours if we remain faithful to Him unto death. The way to perfection is the way of naked faith. It means walking with the Lord in the darkness and at the same time believing in the light (Is. 50:10). There are signposts of perfection which can guide us on our ascent to the holy city. Among these are the commandments of God, the Beatitudes, and the fruits of the Spirit (Gal. 5:22, 23). The law of God as given in Holy Scripture is our norm. But perfection lies in transcending the law through love and thereby fulfilling the law. The way to perfection is different for every person, but the goal is the same, namely, eternal fellowship with Christ.

The attainment of perfection signifies perfect communion with Christ. It represents the fullness of mystical union, that is, union with Christ in glory. Catholic theologians have described this in terms of the beatific vision of God. Evangelical theologians commonly refer to this as glorification. Perfection entails not only union with deity but also union with all of the

---

[15] Martin Luther, *Luther: Lectures on Romans*, ed. W. Pauck, p. 120.

[16] See *Autobiography of St. Thérèse of Lisieux*, trans. Ronald Knox (New York: P. J. Kenedy & Sons, 1958), pp. 98, 248.

glorified saints. It represents therefore not only the transformation of the children of God but a transformed society. The goal of sacred history is not simply personal holiness but social holiness (Wesley). The crown of glory in its broadest sense must be understood as none other than the holy community, the new Jerusalem.

The question concerning the role of good works in the securing of the crown must now be examined. That good works have much bearing on our entry into the kingdom of God is strongly affirmed by Jesus: "Not every one who says to me, 'Lord, Lord,' shall enter the kingdom of heaven, but he who does the will of my Father who is in heaven" (Mt. 7:21; cf. 5:19, 20; 25:31-46).

If we would take into consideration the total biblical witness on this question we must insist that the crown of glory is a free gift of God, not contingent on our striving. Yet this gift is not given apart from the striving of faith (Heb. 12:14). It is given so long as we have faith, although our faith cannot compel God to grant this gift (Wesley). Thomas Aquinas held that we cannot merit final perseverance: therefore the entry into heaven is itself unmerited. The Christian mystics have almost unanimously contended that final salvation must be given by God, although they have insisted that we can do much to prepare ourselves for this salvation.

Yet the Bible does not hesitate to affirm that our good works are rewarded by God. The Psalmist said that God requites a man according to his work (Ps. 62:12). Another Old Testament writer averred that the "one who sows righteousness gets a sure reward" (Prov. 11:18). Jesus stated that when men revile us we should rejoice because our "reward is great in heaven" (Mt. 5:12; cf. Lk. 6:23). He also contended that love for one's enemies will be rewarded (Lk. 6:35). Paul held that authentic works of faith will receive a reward (I Cor. 3:14). In Hebrews we read that the seeking after God will be rewarded (11:6). The First Epistle to Timothy exhorts us to be rich in good deeds, for by so doing we lay up for ourselves a good foundation for the future (6:18, 19).

Roman Catholic theologians have generally held that this

reward is on the basis of our merits. A distinction is commonly drawn in Roman Catholic circles between the merits of congruence (*de congruo*) and the merits of worthiness (*de condigno*). The former refer to works which God rewards because it is fitting or congruous that natural goodness, however inadequate, be rewarded.[17] The merits *de condigno* refer to works that have intrinsic worth and therefore are deserving of a reward. Condign merit springs from both free will and divine grace. Such merit supposes an equality between service and return and is measured by commutative justice. Catholic theologians acknowledge that God is not absolutely obligated to man in any respect, but they insist that in His benevolence He has made it possible for His children to work for and earn their salvation. God has freely bound Himself to reward those works which according to the standards of justice are meritorious or deserving.

Our position is that only the merits of Christ have intrinsic worth, and only these merits can be regarded as the basis for God's acceptance of our works. Insofar as the merits of Christ are inseparable from the mercy of God, we must hold that the rewards spoken of in the Bible concerning good works are rewards not of debt but of grace.[18] Our works are deemed worthy not because of their intrinsic merit but because of God's unmerited grace (Rom. 4:2-5). The rewards of God cannot be based on our merits at all, whether these be merits of congruence or worthiness, because every good work done by sinful man is tainted by sinful intention. Even in those cases where lofty and truly sacrificial motivations are present through the action of the Spirit, they are always accompanied by motivations that are less than pure.

Our works and strivings are accepted by God as wrappings might be accepted for a present. Faith alone lays hold of the crown of life, but faith can bring forward nothing of its own that would insure the gift of final salvation. We simply trust and believe that the crown will be given to us because of the promises of Christ and the mercy of God. At the same time the

17 See explanatory note 23.
18 See explanatory note 24.

crown is not given apart from our faith nor even apart from
our works. The fine linen in which the saints are to be clothed
represents the righteous deeds of the saints (Rev. 19:8). Our
works will adorn us in heaven, but only God's grace can open
the gates into the kingdom. Luther contended that our rewards
determine our place in heaven, but our entry into heaven is
contingent solely upon God's mercy.[19]

What we are saying is that our cooperation with God is not
sufficient to win for us final salvation. Our striving is mixed
with sin and therefore deserves no reward. We must bear fruit
or else faith will wither away; yet our fruit cannot force the
hand of God because it is intertwined with fruit that springs
from doubt and sin. In the sight of God no man is righteous,
not even the greatest saint. Did not an apostle call himself "the
foremost of sinners" (I Tim. 1:15)? As beneficiaries of grace
we can truly cooperate with the Spirit of God, but our cooperation is both positive and negative. By negative cooperation we
mean the kind in which man sets out to do God's will but ends by
actually obstructing this will. Our intention may be positive,
but our performance is woefully inadequate. We are judged
according to our works, but at the same time we are saved in
spite of our works (Tit. 3:4-7). The children of Israel were
given the land of Canaan not because of their righteousness but
because of God's goodness (cf. Deut. 9:4-6). So it is with those
who would inherit the promised land of the kingdom of heaven.
Jesus said that after we have done all, we should acknowledge
that we are unworthy servants (Lk. 17:10). We are unworthy because our faith is weak and our fruit is sparse. If God would
judge us solely in the light of His perfect law, we would all be
condemned by our works. And yet God will not judge us according to our sins but will hearken to our godly fear (Ps. 103:6-
14). We could be condemned by our works, but we will be saved
by our faith. No wonder that Paul can speak of a man being
saved although his work might be rejected (I Cor. 3:14, 15).[20]

---

[19] *Luther's Works*, Vol. 21, ed. J. Pelikan (St. Louis: Concordia, 1956),
pp. 293, 294.

[20] This must not be taken to mean that such a person bore no fruit
whatever, but that much of what he accomplished is not genuine.

No wonder that Peter can refer to the righteous man as being "scarcely saved" (I Pet. 4:18).

Although our works are not meritorious, we must not obscure the fact that they are accepted by God and even rewarded. It is possible for a child of God to do works that are pleasing to Him simply because of the indwelling of God's Spirit. Thus, the credit for our good deeds belongs to God, since it is His Spirit that enables us to do them. Paul's words are very appropriate at this point: "What have you that you did not receive? If then you received it, why do you boast as if it were not a gift?" (I Cor. 4:7). But this should not blind us to the fact that we are being remade in the image of God and that we are being made righteous and worthy by His Spirit (II Thes. 1:5, 11). Our good works cannot gain heaven as a natural right, but they can equip us to enter heaven. At the same time the presence of sin cancels out any merit that we might accumulate, and consequently we shall always come to God as debtors. The Roman Catholic view that we can earn merits above those that we need and that these superabundant merits can be transferred to men less fortunate than we are has absolutely no biblical foundation.[21]

The divine law of justice says that man reaps what he sows (Lk. 6:37, 38; Gal. 6:7). The law of grace says that man reaps beyond what he sows (Mk. 4:24). Man sows imperfection, but he reaps the fruits of perfection, kindness, and charity, not because of his goodness but because of God's mercy. The law of grace is inexplicable apart from the message of faith itself, namely, that Christ reaps what we sow. We have sown rebellion and discord, and Christ reaped the dreaded consequences of this in His death on the cross. He has reaped where He has not sown. Behind all our merits and demerits lies the gracious, unmerited compassion of God, and it is upon this grace and compassion that our salvation rests. John put this very cogently: "In this is love, not that we loved God but that he loved us and sent his Son to be the expiation for our sins" (I Jn. 4:10).

Christ Himself is the prize, the treasure, the crown (cf. Is. 28:5). Christ is the reward that is promised to all men of faith.

21 See explanatory note 25.

And yet in addition to personal fellowship and union with Christ there are also other treasures. When Jesus spoke of treasures in heaven (Mt. 6:20; Mk. 10:21; Lk. 18:22), He was thinking of rewards in the material sense. There is only one prize, but there will be many gifts. There is only one heaven, but in this heaven there are many mansions. We concur with Bonhoeffer's interpretation of this treasure in heaven: "By this treasure Jesus does not mean the one great treasure of himself, but treasures in the literal sense of the word, treasures accumulated by the disciples for themselves."[22] There is a place for treasures and rewards in the Christian faith, but these treasures are to be sought not as ends in themselves but as means to glorify God. Also these treasures are to be viewed as gifts which crown and reward our labors but which God is not obligated to dispense according to the strict law of His justice.

It is now necessary to examine more thoroughly the second advent of Christ and the life hereafter. The second advent signifies the consummation of God's plan of salvation. It represents not simply a revelation of Christ's victory at Calvary (Barth) nor a confirmation of what has already taken place (J. H. Heidegger). Rather, it signifies the fulfillment of what has gone before. The coming again of Christ will usher in a new world, a new heaven and a new earth.

Theologians have long disputed about the state of man between death and the final consummation inaugurated by the second advent of Christ. Our position is that there is an immediate judgment after death which anticipates and foreshadows the final judgment. At the moment of death the souls of men, reclothed in spiritual bodies, are taken either into the presence of God or into the nether land of Sheol, the World of Spirits, where they await the final judgment. Those who die in Christ experience immediately after death the beatific vision of God in Paradise, the realm of the departed saints. The spirits in Sheol or Hades are in a condition of nakedness waiting to be fully clothed at the consummation of world history.[23] But the

---

[22] Dietrich Bonhoeffer, *The Cost of Discipleship*, trans. R. H. Fuller, revised ed. (London: SCM Press, Ltd., 1949), p. 156.
[23] See explanatory note 26.

departed saints also, although clothed in white robes, which
symbolize the resurrection body, wait to be clothed anew with
bodies that are incorruptible and eternal. Although having
attained perfect love and although exempt from the suffering
of sin and death, the glorified saints still suffer vicariously for
their brethren on earth. Their fulfillment depends on the salvation of their struggling brethren in this world. As Hebrews
so poignantly states: ". . . apart from us they should not be made
perfect" (Heb. 11:40). Thomas Aquinas wrote: "The saints in
heaven will have no further need of Christ's atonement; nevertheless, although their atonement be over, they will always need
. . . to be consummated by Christ . . . on whom their glory depends."[24]

The consummation of God's plan of salvation occurs beyond
history rather than within history. The kingdom of God signifies both the *finis* and the *telos* of history — its end in the sense
of time and in the sense of goal. It entails not the annihilation
of the world but rather the transformation of the world into a
new heaven and a new earth. The millennium as described by
Revelation (ch. 20) is symbolic of a period in world history when
the demonic powers will be restrained and God's rule will be
manifest. This period is prior to the general resurrection of the
dead and the second advent of Christ. At the time of the consummation the kingdom of Christ will become the kingdom of
God (I Cor. 15:24) and the church militant, which is the visible
form of Christ's kingdom, will become the church triumphant.
Then those in the nether world and those who have died at the
time of Christ's appearing will be resurrected and brought before the throne of God. Those who are alive at the time of the
parousia (the appearing) will also be brought before the
presence of Christ in order to be judged. This is "the second
resurrection," the first being the resurrection of the departed
saints in past ages.[25]

The last judgment represents the climax of the dramatic

[24] Thomas Aquinas, *Summa Theologica*, Vol. IV, Part III, qu. 22, art. 5,
reply 1 (Paris: Pl. Lethielleux, 1888) , p. 152.
[25] A similar interpretation of the two resurrections is to be found in
Herbert H. Wernecke, *The Book of Revelation Speaks to Us* (Philadelphia:
Westminster Press, 1954) , p. 150.

events at the end of the age. This judgment does not consist simply in the confirmation of the judgment on the cross and the
judgments that take place in our lives and immediately after
death. It signifies also the execution and completion of the
preceding judgments. Those who have opened their hearts to
Christ in faith and repentance will be granted eternal life in
heaven. Even those in the nether world who finally repent and
cast themselves on the mercy of Christ will finally be saved.
Did not Jesus Himself preach to the spirits in prison (I Pet.
3:19; 4:6)?

This brings us to the question of what happens to those
who persist in unbelief. These persons, like the others, will
be judged by their works, but in their case their works are
not accepted because they are rooted in fear and selfishness as
over against faith. The New Testament does not hesitate to
speak of the dreaded reality of hell, the outer darkness where
men will weep and gnash their teeth (Mt. 8:12; 13:42, 50; 25:30;
Lk. 13:28). Paul contended that apart from faith men are separated from Christ and are without God in the world (Eph. 2:
12). Those who are finally banished from the glory of God have
only to blame their own hardness of heart and arrogance. Hell
means exclusion from the joys of heaven and inward torment
caused by the anxiety of guilt and perpetual resistance to grace.

Yet one has not said the last word when he describes hell in
terms of separation and rejection. The New Testament also
speaks of God's all-encompassing love and His will that all men
be saved (cf. Rom. 11:32; Jn. 12:32; I Tim. 2:4; Tit. 2:11).
God's righteousness must always be seen in relationship to His
boundless compassion. To be sure, "judgment is without mercy
to one who has shown no mercy; yet mercy triumphs over judgment" (Jas. 2:13). Again, we must not lose sight of the fact that
Calvary benefits the whole world, not just those who believe.
The cross of Christ has cosmic relevance, and it is to the credit
of Karl Barth that he has reminded us of this fact. We are told
that Christ has overcome and shall finally destroy hell, sin, and
death (I Cor. 15:24-26; Rev. 20:14).

The hell that is the outer darkness is a possibility that has
been crossed out by God, since Christ suffered the torments of

hell in our place. Yet although the real outer darkness has been vanquished, there remains an inner darkness which to unbelievers still appears as an outer darkness. Hell in the sense of total perdition and ontological separation from God has been dealt a deathblow by Christ, but hell in the sense of inner fear and lostness remains. Yet those who persist in rejecting God's love are still claimed by this love. They will be made to glorify God even in their condemnation. They cannot be *sons* of the kingdom, but they are made *servants* of the kingdom even against their wills. They are estranged from the holy community, and yet they are integrally related to this community. They are outside the joy and bliss of the kingdom, but they are within the domain of the kingdom. Hell is a result of God's righteous judgment, but it is at the same time a creation of God's love. In Dante's *The Divine Comedy* hell is marked by a plaque which reads "I too am created by love."

God sanctions hell because in His goodness He wills that there be a place for sinners who reject His love. And yet even the sinners in hell are not outside the compass of God's love. Hell appears to be darkness to the sinner, but darkness is as light to God (Ps. 139:12). Hell means separation from God from the side of the sinner but not from God's side. God is present even in the nether darkness (Ps. 139:7-12; Nah. 1:8), and this accounts for the anguish in hell. To be sure, "Sheol" and the "sea" do not signify the Christian hell, but they are types of the real hell. Certainly the deepest meaning of Psalm 139 is that God is present in every dark and forbidden place. The torments of hell are caused by the fire of God's love that accepts and thereby shames the unacceptable. This fire is also that of divine judgment and wrath; yet as one theologian says, "God's wrath ought not to be misinterpreted as something foreign and contrary to God's love. But one should understand that God's wrath is this burning and consuming love."[26] Hell might therefore aptly be defined as an estrangement within union.

The reason why hell has passed out of theological parlance is that the traditional image of hell is anti-Christian. Hell can-

26 Karl Barth, *A Shorter Commentary on Romans*, trans. D. H. van Daalen (London: SCM Press, Ltd., 1959), p. 26.

not be likened to a concentration camp or torture chamber presided over by the devil, for this would be to posit a co-eternal evil. On the contrary, a biblical picture of hell would be closer to a sanitarium for sick souls presided over not by the devil but by Jesus Christ Himself. The punishment in hell must be regarded as essentially remedial or corrective, not simply as retributive. Man cannot sin against God with impunity, and yet God afflicts the sinner not to annihilate or ruin him but to restrain and correct him. Whether hell is eternal in the sense of everlasting is another question, but it certainly would be consonant with God's love and justice if this were so. Among those who would seem to be hopelessly lost are the sons of perdition, the false prophet, and the devil (cf. Jn. 17:12; II Thes. 2:3-12; Rev. 20: 10). Yet this does not preclude the possibility that some spirits might finally be restored to full health and salvation. The gates of the holy city are depicted as being open day and night (Is. 60:11), and this means that access to the throne of grace is possible continually.

To allow for the possibility of final salvation even for the denizens of hell is not to turn hell into purgatory. Hell is a place where God's purifying fire is present but where it is rejected. The acceptance of God's love always means in the Bible an immediate restoration to grace, and if this should happen in hell we can only conjecture that the sinner then would find himself in heaven. It is well to maintain a healthy agnosticism concerning the final fate of those who are banished to hell, but we can definitely assert that they are in the hands of God. The reason for rejecting the Roman Catholic conception of purgatory is that the crown of glory is no longer viewed as an unmerited gift but as a prize which is withheld from man until he has paid the satisfaction for his transgressions and is thereby made worthy of salvation.

Heaven signifies the fullness of joy and perfect fellowship not only with God but with the whole company of saints. No temple will be found in the heavenly city, since God Himself will be its temple (Rev. 21:22). Heaven is to be regarded as the holy community of love in which the sacred and secular are united in an enduring synthesis.

We are told that there is no marriage in heaven (Mt. 22:30; Lk. 20:35), for the tie that connects the saints is not blood or sex but obedience to God and self-giving love. The kingdom of heaven is a spiritual family, a brotherhood of man under the fatherhood of God. This does not mean that the ties of natural kinship are abrogated in this kingdom, but it does mean that such ties are superseded and transcended. Mothers and fathers, husbands and wives, parents and children, will now see themselves primarily and essentially as brothers and sisters in Christ. Their love for one another is not diminished; on the contrary, it is heightened and raised to a new level. The memory of their past relationships is not forgotten, but they now have fellowship as members of a spiritual family. Just as the relationship of Mary and Jesus took on new significance when she was seen as His spiritual mother, so the relationship among the members of every family that is united in fellowship with Christ will be deepened and transfigured. The fact that the kingdom is already here means that natural bonds are transcended *de jure* among the followers of Christ. But in Paradise and heaven these bonds are superseded and transcended *de facto*. The outward or actual breaking of these bonds can now be seen in the few who embrace vocations that might be deemed "eschatological," that is, monastic and missionary vocations.

Suffering is not present in the kingdom of heaven (Rev. 21:4), despite the fact that men know even as they are known and thus are presumably aware of the existence of hell. The reason is that the saints have the perfect knowledge that all men are taken care of and loved by God. To be sure, God loves His children in a way that is different from His love for those whom He calls "not my people." But God's love is everywhere present and God's rule is everywhere manifest. All things are in God and God is in all things. We can accept with certain modifications Tillich's phrase "eschatological panentheism" as the description of the final consummation of world history. The crown of glory in its deepest sense signifies being with God and being in God as sons of glory.

God desires that all men receive the crown of salvation, and yet God will not grant this reward to faithless and disobedient men. If we would be saved from the hell of abject misery brought about by the rejection of divine love, we must now prepare ourselves to receive this crown. The crown is given despite the inadequacy and insufficiency of our efforts. The crown cannot be merited, nor can it be claimed as a natural right. But if we make no effort at all towards procuring the crown, we will never experience the final joy of salvation. If we fail to bear fruit for the kingdom, the blessing that might have been ours will be withheld from us.

VI

The Christian Pilgrimage

In this chapter an attempt will be made to demonstrate anew the interrelationship of the various dimensions and tenses of salvation. We shall endeavor to confirm the insights of previous chapters that these dimensions are integrally and paradoxically related. This paradoxical relationship will be viewed in the context of the Christian pilgrimage. The Bible testifies throughout that the way to salvation is a way of pilgrimage (cf. Ps. 119: 54; Phil. 3:12-14; Heb. 11:13, 14). It is a way that leads through "the valley of the shadow of death" (Ps. 23:4); the end of our pilgrimage is the "holy hill" (Ps. 43:3), "Mount Zion" (Ps. 48), the city of God.

In the deepest sense our salvation begins and ends in Jesus Christ. The full meaning of the incarnation is that not only God was in Christ but we were in Christ, since Christ is to be seen as the Representative of fallen humanity. In the words of Athanasius, "the Saviour . . . banished death from us and made us anew."[1] Christ dying for us is certainly the foundation and pivotal point of our salvation. Our salvation is carried forward and made concrete in our lives by Christ's dwelling in us. Our salvation will be consummated by Christ's filling us in the state of glory.

Paul makes the three tenses of salvation very clear in Romans 6:22: "But now that you have been set free from sin and have become slaves of God, the return you get is sanctification

---

[1] Athanasius, *The Incarnation of the Word of God*, introd. by C. S. Lewis (New York: Macmillan Co., 1947), p. 44.

and its end, eternal life." When were we set free from sin? Certainly at Calvary, but also in our baptism and conversion, by which the victory of Calvary is appropriated. The victory of Christ becomes more fully realized in our lives in our daily sanctification and is consummated in eternal life.

We can say that our salvation has its source in the free grace of God realized at Calvary; its consummation is fellowship in glory. Another way to put this is that our redemption begins with the incarnation of Jesus Christ at Bethlehem; its end or goal is the glorification of Christ on Mount Zion. In another sense our salvation has its commencement in the covenantal community of the Old Testament; it has its finalization in the holy community which is the kingdom of God. Our restoration is based on the descent of God in Jesus Christ; it is fulfilled in the ascent of the children of God to the holy city. Its foundation is the crucified and risen Christ; its consummation is the triumphant Christ. Its enduring basis is the justification of God; its fulfillment or culmination is the "deification" of man.

As has been said, salvation has not only three basic tenses, but also two poles — objective and subjective. The objective pole is the incarnation of Christ climaxing in His vicarious atonement. The subjective pole is the indwelling of the Spirit culminating in the resurrection of the dead./ Objectively our salvation begins in the mystery of God's love in Jesus Christ; subjectively it commences with our seeking for the help of God. This seeking must of course be viewed as a sign of irresistible grace; otherwise we are in the morass of synergism. That is to say, we could not seek for God unless we had already been found by Him. That man's seeking presupposes the prior action of God is affirmed by Augustine in his *Confessions*:

> But who is there that calls upon Thee without knowing Thee? . . . O Lord, my faith calls on Thee — that faith which Thou hast imparted to me, which Thou hast breathed into me through the incarnation of Thy Son, through the ministry of Thy preacher.[2]

---

[2] Augustine, *The Confessions*, trans. J. G. Pilkington. In *Basic Writings of Saint Augustine*, ed. Whitney J. Oates, Vol. I (New York: Random House, 1948), p. 3.

We have linked man's seeking with irresistible grace rather than prevenient grace because of the latter's associations with synergistic theology. Some theologians (both Roman and Protestant) have postulated a universal prevenient grace by which men are enabled to seek and cooperate with the grace of conversion. Our position is that men cannot begin to seek for the truth of Jesus Christ until they have been grasped by His Spirit in baptism and faith. We would have no objection to the term "prevenient grace" provided that it is not separated from regenerating or saving grace. Prevenient grace should be seen as simply the first step in our regeneration and should always be associated with baptism and the hearing of faith.

The sacrament of baptism attests to the fact that Christ in His church is already seeking us before we seek for Him. When our parents bring us as infants to the church for baptism, we are placed on the road to salvation. Even believers' baptism signifies that God's election precedes human decision, since the believer's decision is a response to the outreaching love of Jesus Christ.

To be sure, if we are born in the covenant community we are claimed for God's kingdom even prior to our baptism. Indeed, we are told that the promises of God are given not only to the people of Zion but to their children (Acts 2:39; cf. I Cor. 7:14). Yet these promises do not generally take concrete effect in our lives until we confess our sins and are baptized (Acts 2:38). It is in the sacrament of baptism that we are turned in the direction of final salvation.

Baptism might therefore be regarded as the narrow gate. It sets us on the straight way which leads to the eternal city. The baptismal rite is the symbol of the new birth. It is the effectual sign of regeneration (Acts 22:16; Eph. 5:26; Titus 3:5). It testifies to and effectuates our death in Christ (Rom. 6:3f.; Col. 2:12).

Yet baptism must not be separated from the decision of faith. We cannot accept the Catholic conception of *ex opere operato,* if this is taken to mean that the rite in and of itself effects salvation. On the other hand, if this means, as some Roman Catholic scholars believe, that it is Christ who brings about salvation through this rite, then we have no objection.[3]

We can adhere to the Reformed principle of *nullum sacramentum sine fide* (no sacrament without faith) provided that this does not make the presence of Christ in the sacrament depend upon the faith of the recipient. Christ is objectively present in baptism, even in sectarian baptism (as Augustine maintained) ; yet the work of Christ is ineffectual where there is no contrition and faith. We could subscribe to the view of the Roman Catholic Thomas Merton, who writes that "the sacramental system is objective in its operation, but grace is not communicated to one who is not properly disposed. The saccraments produce no fruit where there is no love."[4]

The complex and paradoxical relationship between baptism and faith has been a source of theological controversy through the ages. Wesley is probably as correct as anyone when he affirms that although the new birth is begun in baptism it is not fulfilled until the experience of faith.[5] However, we must point out that this refers only to the general pattern of Christian experience. In Paul's case baptism succeeded the decision. Yet Paul did not receive the Spirit until his baptism (Acts 9:17, 18) . In the case of the Samaritans (Acts 8:4-22) their new birth did not occur until shortly after their baptism, even though they believed at the time of baptism. Most scholars hold that they did not have true faith, since they had not yet repented.[6] They had believed with their minds (*credentia*) but not with their hearts (*fiducia*) .

Theologians are nearest the truth when they affirm that

---

3 See Godfrey Diekmann's essay in Peter Bartholome, *et al.*, *Christians in Conversation* (Westminster: Newman Press, 1962) . Diekmann maintains that the phrase *ex opere operato* really means *ex opere Christi*, "by the action of Christ." See p. 93. A similar view is held by E. Schillebeeckx in his *Christ the Sacrament of the Encounter with God* (New York: Sheed & Ward, 1963) , pp. 69-73; 82-89.

4 Thomas Merton, *Life and Holiness* (New York: Herder & Herder, 1963) , p. 79.

5 See Colin Williams, *John Wesley's Theology Today* (Nashville: Abingdon Press, 1960) , pp. 115-122.

6 The text seems to indicate that they had believed in Philip because of the signs and wonders that he accomplished. Simon also believed in Philip's message, but yet he had not forsaken his sins (8:22) .

one is incorporated into the church by both baptism and faith. We are made Christians by "water and the Spirit" (Jn. 3:5). The decision of faith is not a second baptism of the Spirit after the baptism with water, but simply the climax of the one movement of the Spirit which begins (or ends) in baptism with water.

It must be acknowledged that when baptism with water is administered in the community of faith it is always related to Spirit-baptism, whereas Spirit-baptism is not in every case directly connected to baptism with water. Sacramental baptism is generally necessary for salvation, but only faith — the creation of the Spirit — is indispensable. The inner reality is the most important thing, and yet the inner reality has been united with an outward form by the word of Christ.

That baptism is often necessary for those who have made a decision for Christ and are not yet baptized is attested by the following report from the mission field in India given by D. T. Niles.[7] This missionary writes of a Hindu doctor who was converted to Christianity but who postponed his baptism. Finally under pressure from his friends and family he gave up the idea of baptism and fell back into the old religion. He had made a personal commitment of faith, and yet the harvest was lost. His new birth was aborted because he refused to be baptized into the body of Christ.

Baptism is a first step on the road to salvation, but it is only a preliminary step (even in the case of believers' baptism). Our objection to many theories of baptismal regeneration is that they presuppose that regeneration is consummated at baptism. Luther had some wise words on this point:

> But we should note that it is not necessary that all be found in this state of perfection as soon as they are baptized into this kind of death. For they are baptized "into death," i.e., toward death; in other words: they have taken only the first steps toward the attainment of this death as their goal.[8]

7 Daniel T. Niles, *The Context In Which We Preach* (Geneva: John Knox House Association, 1956), p. 11.

8 Martin Luther, *Luther: Lectures on Romans*, ed. and trans. W. Pauck (Philadelphia: Westminster Press, 1961), p. 181.

If we are to remain on the straight way on which baptism places us, then we must take up the cross and bear the cross. We must seek to become like Christ in His death (Phil. 3:10). We must strive to live a life of obedient decision. We must seek to die with Christ. We must bear the cross in faithfulness and thanksgiving. We must bring forth fruit with patience (Lk. 8:15). We must hold fast to the Word and keep the Word (Rev. 3:10; Lk. 11:28). The way to Mount Zion is depicted as "the Holy Way" (Is. 35:8). The unclean shall not pass over it, and therefore we must seek to be holy even as God is holy (Lev. 19:2; I Pet. 1:15, 16).

At the moment of decision we take up the cross placed upon us at baptism. Baptism is a sign both of our election and our response or decision. Confirmation is a sign of our consecration as we face our responsibilities in the world. Confirmation supplements but does not complete baptism. It should be regarded as a commissioning to Christian service. It signifies the decision that determines the direction of our vocation in the world. Ordination, matrimony, and sacramental confession renew and deepen what has already taken place in baptism. These rites, like confirmation, can be regarded as veritable means of grace but not as sacraments. They can be viewed as "sacramental," but Reformed theology has wisely reserved the term "sacrament" for those two rites which have been explicitly commanded by Christ for our salvation. Confirmation, ordination, matrimony, and other rites strengthen us in faith, but they do not bring us faith.

Those who stand in the Holiness and Pentecostal traditions have held that baptism and conversion must be fulfilled in the experience of Pentecost or "entire sanctification." This experience has also been called the "second blessing," "the baptism of the Holy Spirit," "the sealing of the Spirit," and the "Pentecostal infilling." Such a belief manifests a deep misunderstanding.[9] The decision of faith must be viewed as nothing other

---

[9] Some who stand in this tradition speak of the threefold blessing of the Spirit, which is signified by conversion, sanctification, and Spirit-baptism. The Pentecostal Holiness Church, for example, divides its members into three classes — the saved, the sanctified, and the Spirit-baptized.

than the baptism of the Spirit. Did not Peter contend that faith itself effects cleansing or regeneration (Acts 15:9)? The experience of Pentecost is inseparable from the experience of Calvary. We cannot receive Christ without at the same time receiving the Spirit. In Paul's mind those who are in the Spirit are the same as those who are in Christ (Rom. 8:9-11; I Cor. 12:12, 13; II Cor. 3:17; Eph. 4:4-6).

The truth in the Holiness position is that salvation consists in more than simply one decision. Our union with Christ and His Spirit must be continually renewed and deepened. Our sanctification by the Spirit is a lifelong process that ends only at death. The Christian life is not simply a decision for Christ but a participation in His sufferings. We shall finally enter the kingdom only through many tribulations (Acts 14:22), and this means that the pilgrim way is not an easy one.

The sacrament of the Lord's Supper was given to us as a means by which we are enabled to remain on the path to salvation. It is a means by which we receive strength to continue the struggle of faith. We are set on the way at baptism; we are kept on the way by Holy Communion. In a wider sense we are kept on the way by all the means of grace — preaching, devotional reading, confession, prayer, instruction, and the like. Yet the sacrament of the Lord's Supper has certainly a special place among the means of salvation, for here we are confronted by the *real presence* of Christ. In this sacrament we are renewed in the faith in a special way. Yet even the Lord's Supper does not benefit us apart from our repentance and faithful obedience.

The truth is that there are no external nor experiential guarantees for our salvation. Baptism by itself is certainly not sufficient for full regeneration. Being born into the covenant does not assure us of salvation. The experience of the new birth is no absolute guarantee or security. The decision of faith is not enough, although this is sometimes the impression given by modern revivalists. Neither is confirmation or a rite of sealing the key to final salvation.[10]

10 A few sects, for example, the New Apostolic Church, make the sacrament of sealing (*Versiegelung*), which corresponds to the Catholic sacrament of confirmation, indispensable for salvation. This is why even the dead are "sealed" by proxy. The Mormons have a similar doctrine.

Because there are no external securities in the Christian life, our baptism must be renewed daily. We must lay hold of and recover the grace of baptism ever again.[11] In the words of an early Puritan divine: "The Christian life is made up of ever new beginnings."[12] That is to say, we are to remain true to our baptism by a life of service and sacrifice. We must pray without ceasing. We must come again and again to the table of the Lord and feed upon the living bread that nourishes and strengthens us for kingdom service.

According to Roman Catholic doctrine baptism saves from original sin, but a second sacrament, penance, is necessary to save us from actual sins or sins committed after baptism. Penance is consequently a "second plank" in our salvation (Tertullian). The Protestant Reformers (Luther in particular) inveighed against this idea of a second plank and held that baptism saves from all sin if we remain true to our baptism. What is needed is not the so-called sacrament of penance but daily repentance under the cross.[13] In a deeper sense we must return not to our baptism alone but to Calvary, for Calvary is the event where our salvation was fought for and won. There is still a place for sacramental confession in evangelical church life, but this confession must not be viewed as a means of satisfaction for sin. Rather, it must be seen as a practical means of appropriating the assurance of pardon.

In the circles of evangelical revivalism the experience of conversion overshadows baptism. At our conversion, it is alleged, we are saved from mortal sins and thereby made regenerate or "holy." As has already been mentioned, in Holiness groups it is believed that a second crisis experience after conversion brings

[11] Cf. Emil Brunner: "We have already been baptized as children in this name but this baptism is useless to us if it is not accepted in faith again and again." *I Believe in the Living God,* trans. and ed. John Holden (Philadelphia: Westminster Press, 1961), p. 117.

[12] Quoted in John Baillie, *Baptism and Conversion* (London: Oxford University Press, 1964), p. 106.

[13] Luther sometimes spoke of repentance as a second sacrament. But by this he always meant a confirmation of baptism. This separation of penance and regeneration is not to be found in Calvin.

us full sanctification. The sins after this experience are regarded as "faults" and are not seen as condemnatory. In our view the Christian is at all times threatened by sin, and he continually succumbs to sinful temptation. His hopes lie not in some new crisis experience or some additional sacrament (such as penance) but rather in daily repentance. Even his smallest sin becomes "mortal" unless he repents of it.

This is not to imply that we are necessarily opposed to revivalism as such. There may very well be a place for an altar call or an invitation to a public decision at certain times in the church year. The call should probably be given by a visiting evangelist rather than the pastor, but this depends on the special gifts of the pastor. At the same time it should be made clear that baptized believers are being called to confirm their baptismal vows rather than be baptized anew by the Spirit. Another way to meet the need for a public declaration of faith is the restoration of the weekly celebration of Holy Communion, in which people are called to go publicly to the altar to partake of the body and blood of Christ. One reason why the altar call has become so important among conservative evangelicals is that the significance of the sacrament of the altar has generally been lost sight of in their churches.

The early history of Israel can be regarded as a pattern or type of the Christian pilgrimage. Just as the children of Israel were in bondage in Egypt, so the members of the church have been in bondage to sin. The deliverance of the people of Israel through the Red Sea can be viewed as a foreshadowing of the deliverance of mankind through water and the Spirit (cf. I Cor. 10:1-4). Just as the Red Sea typifies the narrow gate, so Mount Sinai is the symbol of the straight way. The Torah (law) served as the moral norm for the children of Israel; *agape* love serves as the final norm for the New Israel. The pillar of fire is a type of the guidance of the Holy Spirit in the church. The manna given to the Israelites in the wilderness is a type of the Bread of Life given in Word and sacrament (cf. Jn. 6:31-34). The manna and the water in the rock are certainly parallel to the Eucharist. The crossing of the Jordan symbolizes the transition from this life to the life to come.[14]

Jesus saw His own life and the lives of His disciples as a re-enactment of the pilgrimage of the Jews. He recapitulated the pilgrimage of Israel as a sign of His role as the suffering serv-ant.[15] He believed that His work as priest, prophet, and king was the fulfillment of those particular ministries in the history of Israel. The itinerant ministry of His disciples was likened to the going forth of the children of Israel into the wilderness. His journey to Jerusalem is to be seen as a partial fulfillment of the eschatological return of the people of Israel to the holy city.[16]

The life and pilgrimage of Jesus can certainly be viewed as a pattern for the Christian in every age. The Virgin Birth of Jesus is a type of the new birth. The baptism of Jesus must be seen as the moment of His consecration for service to the world. It also can be regarded as a sign of His election, which in His case was realized at His birth. The temptations that Jesus experienced are similar to those experienced by all Chris-tians. His ministry of service to the outcasts and the poor is a model for every Christian ministry. His passion and death point to the fact that vicarious suffering is the key to the victorious life. His resurrection corresponds to the experience of the new life in Christ. The travail of Jesus in Gethsemane foreshadows the mystical night, which is one of the higher stages of the pil-grimage of faith.

The life of Jesus is the pattern for the Christian pilgrimage, but our pilgrimage is not the very same as His. There is no literal reduplication of His life and sufferings, for this would turn the Christian into a second Saviour. Against Reid we must insist that there is no point-to-point correspondence be-

[14] In perfectionist theologies the crossing of the Jordan is most often interpreted as a type of the experience of perfection, and the conquest of Canaan is associated with the victorious life. Cf. Theodore Hegre, *The Will of God Your Sanctification* (Minneapolis: Bethany Fellowship, 1961), pp. 78-80.

[15] See E. J. Tinsley, *The Imitation of God in Christ* (Philadelphia: West-minster Press, 1960), pp. 67-99.

[16] *Ibid.*, p. 83.

tween our pilgrimage and tribulations and His.[17] The pilgrimage of the disciple mirrors and proclaims the pilgrimage of the Saviour, but it does not reduplicate or recreate this pilgrimage. The Christian pilgrimage is the way of daily repentance. It signifies the continual dying of the old man and the renewing of the new. This is certainly Calvin's position:

> Therefore, I think he has profited greatly who has learned to be very much displeased with himself, not so as to stick fast in this mire and progress no farther, but rather to hasten to God and yearn for him in order that, having been engrafted into the life and death of Christ, he may give attention to continual repentance.[18]

Jonathan Edwards reminds us that the converted man must also be converted.[19] Luther was fond of quoting Revelation 22:11: "He that is righteous, let him be righteous still" (KJ).

This brings us again to the doctrine of conversion. As has been said, conversion in the deepest sense means lifelong struggle. Its ground is the sacrificial death of Jesus Christ (cf. Rom. 6:6). Its seed is the sacrament of Holy Baptism. Its realization takes place in the decision of faith. Its progression and consummation are to be viewed in conjunction with the obedience and perseverance of the Christian. Although conversion entails a first decision for Christ, it basically refers to a lifelong process of restoration. In the New Testament the words for "convert" (*metanoeo, epistrepho*) can signify a turning again to God as well as a first decision (cf. Lk. 17:3, 4; 22:32; Rev. 2:5, 16, 21; 3:19). On the part of those who have been baptized as infants and who have been nurtured in a Christian home, conversion represents an awakening to the work of the Holy Spirit within them rather than a first coming of the Spirit. The dynamic and continuous nature of conversion is underlined by Thomas Merton:

> It is perfectly true that we die with him in baptism and rise from the dead: but this is only the beginning of a series of deaths and

---

[17] See J. K. S. Reid, *Our Life in Christ* (Philadelphia: Westminster Press, 1963), p. 127.

[18] John Calvin, *Institutes of the Christian Religion*, III, 3, 20, p. 615.

[19] See John Gerstner, *Steps to Salvation* (Philadelphia: Westminster Press, 1960), pp. 156, 157.

resurrections. We are not "converted" only once in our life but many times, and this endless series of large and small "conversions," inner revolutions, leads finally to our transformation in Christ.[20]

Yet although conversion is essentially a process which continues through life, it almost always involves a definite break with the past, and sometimes this break is very dramatic. Those who have fallen away from their baptism and those who are completely outside the church need to be turned drastically in an altogether new direction. Brunner's words are very appropriate in this connection:

> Perhaps you bear in memory the time when it first happened; but there are many who cannot be definite about the "first time" who nevertheless know that it *has* happened, and happens every day. But there is another possibility, perhaps it has *never* happened to you! In that event that seemingly arrogant question, "Are you converted?" is, indeed, not so improper after all.[21]

The pilgrimage of faith and conversion cannot be fully understood apart from the perseverance of the saints. As the apostle said: "For we share in Christ, if only we hold our first confidence firm to the end . . ." (Heb. 3:14; cf. Mt. 10:22; Lk. 21:19; Rom. 8:17; I Cor. 9:24-27; Phil. 3:8-14). Perseverance is not simply an effect or fruit of our justification; it is the means and the condition for the fulfillment of the promises of justification. This was certainly the view of Jonathan Edwards: "Perseverance is not only a necessary concomitant and evidence of a title to salvation but also a necessary prerequisite to the actual possession of eternal life."[22] The culmination and reward of perseverance is the crown of righteousness that is given to all those who have "finished the race" and "kept the faith" (II Tim. 4:7, 8).

That there is a possibility of real progress in the Christian life is certainly affirmed in Scripture (cf. II Thes. 1:3; Phil. 1: 25). The pilgrimage of faith leads to ever greater sanctification on the part of those who seek their security ever again in Jesus

---

20 Thomas Merton, *Life and Holiness,* pp. 158, 159.
21 Emil Brunner, *Our Faith,* trans. John W. Rilling (New York: Charles Scribner's Sons, 1954), p. 102.
22 Jonathan Edwards, "Sermon on Job 27:10" in *The Works of President Edwards,* Vol. VI (New York: G. & C. & H. Carvill, 1830), p. 84.

Christ. Yet our progress is not unbroken but uneven and inter-
mittent. We constantly fall back, but we must strive to rise
again and recover what we have lost. If we refuse to rise again
and push forward, then we shall retrogress. In Luther's words:

> For not he that starts to seek but he that "perseveres" in seeking
> . . . will be saved . . . one who begins his seeking all over again,
> ever seeking again what he has found. For he that does not go
> forward in God's way goes backward. And he that does not
> persist in seeking loses what he has found, for there is no stand-
> ing still in the way of God.[23]

It was Luther's view that the degree of our progress by no means
determines our standing in the sight of God, since our justification is to be attributed to faith alone. On the other hand, if
we cease to make progress and begin to fall away from faith itself, our standing before God will be imperiled.

Growth in sanctification entails not only a deeper communion
with the Spirit but an increase in personal piety.[24] Paul maintained that we "are being changed into his likeness from one
degree of glory to another" (II Cor. 3:18). We can make progress not only *in* our justification and sanctification but also
toward justification and sanctification, in that perfection is the
fulfillment and goal (*telos*) of both.

Sanctity might be considered the positive side of our progress,
the consciousness of sin the negative side; joy is the positive side,
suffering the negative. Calvin and Luther stressed the negative
side of our sanctification. The further we progress in our pilgrimage the deeper becomes our awareness of our sinfulness and
helplessness. Francis of Assisi and John Wesley emphasized
the positive aspects of sanctification. They rightly remind us
that pilgrimage entails not only sin-consciousness and repentance but also inward triumph over sin and outgoing love to our
neighbor. We would not be far wrong in our understanding

23 Martin Luther, *Luther: Lectures on Romans,* ed. Wilhelm Pauck, p. 91.
24 The relation between sanctification and empirical piety has been a
constant source of controversy in Lutheran theology. Holl and Seeburg
have argued that growth in sanctification means a growth in empirical piety.
Prenter takes an opposite position. See Regin Prenter, *Spiritus Creator,*
trans. John M. Jensen (Philadelphia: Muhlenberg Press, 1953), pp. 69, 96f.,
181f.

of the sanctified life by describing it in terms of anguished joy
and comforted despair (Luther).

The sanctity or holiness that is in Christ is imputed to every-
one who has faith. We also hold that all Christians begin to
partake of this holiness in fact or else their belief is only opinion
and not real faith. At the same time only a few Christians actually realize this sanctity to an extraordinary degree in their
lives. Consequently there might be a place for "saints" in the
special sense of this word in evangelical piety. Only a few
mirror and reveal the holiness of Christ before the world. At
the same time it must be insisted upon that the *extraordinarius*
is no more worthy in the sight of God than other Christians.
His holiness is not something that he has accomplished; rather,
his holiness is symbolic — it points beyond itself to Jesus Christ,
who alone is holy in the full sense of this word. The "saint"
is one who witnesses to the presence of the Holy rather than one
who has arrived at holiness. In Tillich's view the "saint" or
the "image of perfection" is not only directed towards the divine but also constantly threatened by the demonic: "The image of perfection is the man who, on the battlefield between
the divine and the demonic, prevails against the demonic,
though fragmentarily and in anticipation."[25]

In this connection it is well for us to consider the relation
between alien (imputed) righteousness (cf. Phil. 3:8f.) and
actual or essential righteousness. Prenter argues in his book
Spiritus Creator that we are justified only by the former, that is,
by the righteousness of Christ. We are covered by the righteousness of Christ, but we remain sinners. He acknowledges that
faith is never without the expulsion of sin, but he holds that
there is no actual progression towards personal holiness. The
Spirit begins to expel sin in our lives, but we lapse into new sin
continually. According to Prenter sanctification is a circular
movement whereby we begin and end in the state of faith as
over against an ascent towards perfection. Sanctification is the
"repeated putting to death of self" and not "a gradually in-

[25] Paul Tillich, *Systematic Theology*, III (Chicago: University of Chicago
Press, 1963), p. 241.

creasing real righteousness."[26] Reinhold Niebuhr reflects a similar point of view when he maintains that we are divinely redeemed in principle but not in fact.[27]

Although it is true that our justification is logically prior to our sanctification, this certainly does not mean that we are left in our sin. Are we not actually changed internally? Is not the man in Christ "a new creation" (II Cor. 5:17)? Both Calvin and Luther spoke of being engrafted into the righteousness of Christ, and this truth must not be obscured. Although they were reluctant to speak of infused grace (*gratia infusa*), they nevertheless held that grace understood as divine favor and mercy has concrete effects in the lives of men. Alien righteousness signifies the fire of the presence of God; actual or empirical righteousness is to be equated with the glow that results from an encounter with that divine fire. Our salvation is anchored in the uncreated light of Christ, but true Christians will manifest this light before the world (Mt. 5:14-16). Did not Jesus say: "You will know them by their fruits" (Mt. 7:16; cf. Jn. 13:35)? Consequently we must hold that empirical piety is an authentic sign of our justification.

We concur in the Reformation view that only the righteousness of Christ justifies us. Only Christ is the "new man" in the full sense of this term; we are still on the way to becoming new men. In Christ we are holy, but in ourselves we remain sinners. Yet this is only part of the truth. We are called to become what we already are in Christ. We are called to attain to the "measure of the stature of the fulness of Christ" (Eph. 4:13). We can and do make progress. Calvin wrote that every Christian should "proceed according to the measure of his . . . capacity" and thereby register some small degree of "progress in the way of the Lord."[28]

The righteousness of Christ is not only imputed to us but also implanted within us. Because of this fact we can do real works of piety and grace. Indeed, in one sense sin is now the

---

26 Regin Prenter, *Spiritus Creator*, pp. 87, 245.

27 See Reinhold Niebuhr, *The Nature and Destiny of Man* (New York: Charles Scribner's Sons, 1951), Vol. II, pp. 49, 87, 121, 137, 230, 243. See also explanatory note 27.

28 Calvin, *Institutes*, III, 7, 5, p. 689.

alien element within the Christian, whereas Christ is now the ground and center of our nature. The man in Christ is no longer paralyzed by sin nor is he under the control of sin. There are no longer two men within us; rather, there is one man — the forgiven sinner who is on the way to being made righteous.

It is high time that the debate between the Calvinists, who uphold progressive sanctification, and the Wesleyans, who defend entire sanctification, be resolved. It is possible and indeed imperative to uphold both of these truths. Entire sanctification is our goal and standard. It can be anticipated fragmentarily and brokenly in this life. One can be lifted above sin in moments, but one is never placed in a state of sinless perfection. Progressive sanctification is the means to the goal of Christian perfection or entire sanctification. Calvin placed the accent on progressive sanctification; yet he earnestly upheld the ideal of evangelical perfection:

> I do not insist that the moral life of a Christian man breathe nothing but the very gospel, yet this ought to be desired, and we must strive toward it. . . . Let that target be set before our eyes at which we are earnestly to aim. Let that goal be appointed toward which we should strive and struggle.[29]

Yet despite the fact that he makes a place for evangelical perfection, Calvin conceives of the Christian life much more in terms of struggle and striving as over against conquest. Calvinism has never perceived the heights of sanctity that are open to the Christian, although it has talked much of sanctification. The classical Calvinist sees the Christian as struggling in the valley rather than advancing up the mountain towards the pinnacle of perfection.

On the other hand, the Wesleyans have not always succeeded in avoiding the pitfall of perfectionism, the view that the perfection which Christ demands can be fully attained in this life. Our position is that the Christian is never in a state of perfection but that he is continually being grasped by perfection itself. That Wesley basically held to a dynamic conception of holiness is attested in the following statement:

29 *Ibid.*, III, 6, 5, p. 688.

> They [Christians] have power to overcome all these enemies; for "sin hath no more dominion over them"; but it is not from nature, either in whole or in part; it is the mere gift of God; nor is it given all at once, as if they had a stock laid up for many years; but from moment to moment.[30]

We maintain that Scriptural holiness can be an experienced reality in the lives of men although perfection in its fullness constantly eludes them. The close relationship between personal holiness and the pilgrimage of faith is well expressed by Stephen Neill:

> Christian holiness, whether for the Church or for the individual, can never be a static thing, something gained once for all. It has to be maintained amid conflicts and perils that are renewed day by day. It is a moving thing; it can only exist as a function of pilgrimage.[31]

In summary, the alien righteousness of Christ is the basis on which we gain entry to heaven. At the same time personal holiness is also necessary, not to entitle us to heaven, but to prepare us for the benefits of heaven. Only those who become holy in their earthly lives are enabled to lay hold of and appreciate the glory of the kingdom. Wesley made this very clear:

> The righteousness of Christ is doubtless necessary for any soul that enters into glory. But so is personal holiness too, for every child of a man. But it is highly needful to be observed that they are necessary in different respects. The former is necessary to *entitle* us to heaven; the latter to *qualify* us for it. Without the righteousness of Christ, we could have no *claim* to glory; without holiness we could have no *fitness* for it.[32]

The consummation of the pilgrimage of faith, the end of the road is none other than the holy city, the *polis,* not the *ecclesia.* The holy city signifies the crown of our justification and sanctification. When the Chief Shepherd is manifested, we shall obtain this unfading crown (I Pet. 5:4). But we shall obtain it

---

30 John Wesley, *Wesley's Standard Sermons,* ed. Edward H. Sugden, Vol. II (London: Epworth Press, 1921), p. 389.

31 Stephen Neill, *Christian Holiness* (New York: Harper & Bros., 1960), p. 112.

32 *The Works of John Wesley,* Vol. VII (Grand Rapids: Zondervan Publishing House, n.d.), Sermon CXX, p. 314.

not on the basis of holiness or works (which are imperfect) but on the basis of free grace. At the time of our glorification Jesus Christ also will be glorified. To be sure, He was already glorified in His resurrection and ascension. But He shall be glorified anew "in his saints" (II Thes. 1:10).

We can experience now our future perfection. The "already" is present in the "not yet." This is the truth in the theology of glory (*theologia gloriae*). Indeed, we are already drawn "into his marvelous light" (I Pet. 2:9). We already sit "in the heavenly places" (Eph. 2:6). Now we have the "first fruits" of the Spirit. According to Calvin we experience not only mortification of the flesh but also vivification of the spirit. This is the pledge of the glory that is still to be revealed to us.

Yet there is another side to faith. God appears to be absent. The Christian is compelled to believe even against his experience. He is divested of outward supports and securities. That is to say, there is not only an experiential element in faith but also a desert element. Certainly Jesus in Gethsemane experienced this dark night of faith. Luther regarded this stage of faith as the highest point in the Christian pilgrimage:

> This is real strength, to trust in God when to all our senses and reason He appears to be angry; and to have greater confidence in Him than we feel. . . . Beyond all this is the highest stage of faith, when God punishes the conscience not only with temporal sufferings, but with death, hell, and sin, and refuses grace and mercy, as though it were His will to condemn and be angry eternally.[33]

Christian mystics have described this as a state of aridity. It does not mean that God is absent, but that He is so near that His presence blinds the senses. This state of aridity, where God appears to withdraw, is not to be confused with the state of lukewarmness, where God actually withdraws. John of the Cross described the arid periods in the life of the Christian as "the dark night of the senses" and "the dark night of the soul." He held that God is present in such periods but that He is hidden. In the theology of this Spanish mystic the dark night

[33] *Works of Martin Luther*, Vol. I (Philadelphia: A. J. Holman Co., 1915), pp. 192, 193.

of the soul is the first level in the stage of union which signifies the culmination of the mystical ascent.

The further we progress in the life of faith the more we are compelled to walk in the darkness. The children in the faith often have to have experiential supports and crutches. They have a special need to feel the glow of the Spirit. But the fathers in the faith walk by pure faith without reliance upon outward signs and crutches. The most authentic theology is the theology of the cross (*theologia crucis*). This means to walk and live under the cross, waiting for the glory that is still withheld from us. Elizabeth Clephane pointed to this truth in her hymn "Beneath the Cross of Jesus": "I take, O cross, Thy shadow / For my abiding place; / I ask no other sunshine than / The sunshine of His face."

Yet we must not ignore the truth in the theology of glory that Christ is present with us now through His Spirit. Indeed, we believe not only in His crucifixion but also in His resurrection. Our future glory can break into our present darkness. One medieval mystic speaks of "a shaft of spiritual light, which pierces this cloud of unknowing between you, and shows you some of his secrets, of which it is not permissible or possible to speak."[34] The author continues: "Then will you feel your affection flame with the fire of his love, far more than I can possibly say now." That is, the mystical union can be felt as well as believed. Even the vision of God can be experienced in this life (cf. Stephen and Paul) but not in its entirety. The beatific vision in its fullness can be known only after death.

The condition of the Christian is one of becoming. The victorious life is a striving towards victory rather than a matured possession of victory. The life of faith is a life of conflict and struggle. It consists in certainty in the midst of uncertainty. We have now a foretaste of our future perfection. We can experience now our coming glory. But against every form of religious enthusiasm we hold that this glory and perfection cannot

---

[34] *The Cloud of Unknowing*, ed. and trans. Clifton Wolters (Baltimore: Penguin Books, 1961), p. 87.

be possessed in this life.[35] Now we must walk by faith, not by sight.

There is much truth in Luther's view that the Christian is justified and at the same time a sinner (*simul peccator ac iustus*). The child of God is in a state of sin as well as of grace. Luther put this very poignantly:

> Man is always in the condition of nakedness, always in the state of potentiality, always in the condition of activity. He is always in sin and always in justification. He is always a sinner, but also always repentant and so always righteous.[36]

Yet Luther's view can give rise to misconceptions. Many theologians have understood *simul peccator ac iustus* as meaning that grace is imputed to us, but sin remains our actual state. The truth is, however, that the state of sin is behind us; the state of grace is before us. The condition of being bound is our past, not our present, and certainly not our future. It is better to say that the Christian is now rooted and grounded in grace, although he is still afflicted by sin. Calvin maintained that unbelief does not assail the Christian from without but from within.[37] Luther stated that the head of the serpent has been crushed, but his slimy scales remain.[38] That is to say, the root of bitterness is taken away when we become children of light; yet the pangs of bitterness are not yet extinguished.

The condition of the new man in Christ can be made clear by comparing it to a transplanted tree. The Christian is like a dying tree which has been taken out of stony ground and replanted in good soil. The Christian is no longer in sin because he is now rooted in the life of Christ. However, he is not yet in glory because he still finds himself in a weakened condition. The tree has not yet been nourished back to health and

---

[35] See explanatory note 28.

[36] M. Luther, *Commentary on the Epistle to the Romans*, trans. J. Theodore Mueller (Grand Rapids: Zondervan Publishing House, 1954) , p. 152. In his *Commentary on Galatians* Luther phrased this in the following way: "Thus a Christian man is righteous and a sinner at the same time, holy and profane, an enemy of God and a child of God." *Luther's Works*, Vol. 26, ed. J. Pelikan (St. Louis: Concordia, 1963) , p. 232.

[37] John Calvin, *Institutes*, III, 2, 21, p. 567.

[38] Martin Luther, *Luther's Works*, Vol. 26, ed. J. Pelikan, p. 189.

appears to be still sick and scrawny. Only if the tree bears fruit can one determine whether the transplanting has been a success.

The Christian need not fall into sin because he is now united with Christ. Yet he does fall ever again because of the aberrant desire to return to his past, a desire which leaves the door open for the re-entry of sin. This does not explain why we yield to this desire because we have the power not to yield. This is why Barth calls sin "an impossible possibility." In Christ the child of God cannot sin (*non posse peccare*) (I Jn. 3:9), but outside of Christ he can do nothing but sin. The Christian is grounded in Christ, but the mystery is that he falls away from his ground ever again. Yet his spiritual life (Christ) continues to exist even when he falls away, so long as he does not renounce his faith altogether.

Our theology is one of wayfarers (*theologia viatorum*). The Christian is on the way, but he has not yet arrived. The old man has been drowned at baptism, but he continues to bob up to the surface (Luther). We are still sick although we are in the process of being healed. We are making progress and the end is in view (Heb. 11:13). The new age has already dawned; the darkness is passing away (I Jn. 2:8). Yet we await the full light of day. We still walk by a pillar of fire at night and by a cloud in the daytime. The light that is now shining is veiled by a "cloud of unknowing." Therefore our pilgrimage must be based upon faith alone and not upon the illumination that we can gain from our senses. Our pilgrimage will end only when the veil is taken away and we see God face to face. Then we shall know even as we are now known (I Cor. 13:12). But in the meantime we are strangers and exiles seeking a country that can be called our own (Heb. 11:13). We continue on this pilgrimage only because we believe in the promises of God.

VII

The Paradox of Salvation

The paradox of salvation expresses the coincidence of divine and human freedom. It points to the truth that man is most free when he is most dependent and most obedient. Indeed, it can be said that man is wholly free when he is wholly persuaded and fully empowered. Man's obedience can therefore be considered voluntary and at the same time a sign and means of God's election. John Chrysostom expressed the paradox when he said: "Now he that draws draws him who wishes to be drawn."[1] St. Paul voiced this paradox in I Corinthians 15:10: "But by the grace of God I am what I am, and his grace toward me was not in vain. On the contrary, I worked harder than any of them, though it was not I, but the grace of God which is with me" (cf. Phil. 2:12, 13; Gal. 2:20).

The mystery of the conjunction of God's grace and man's faithful response has been echoed in several of the Reformation and post-Reformation confessions. But the most cogent statement of this paradox, in our estimation, is that of the Westminster Confession:

> Their ability to do good works is not at all of themselves, but wholly from the Spirit of Christ. And that they may be enabled thereunto, besides the graces they have already received, there is required an actual influence of the same Holy Spirit to work in them to will and to do of his good pleasure; yet are they not hereupon to grow negligent, as if they were not bound to per-

Grace

---

[1] Quoted in J. K. S. Reid, *Our Life in Christ* (Philadelphia: Westminster Press, 1963) , p. 114.

127

form any duty unless upon a special motion of the Spirit; but
they ought to be diligent in stirring up the grace of God that
is in them.[2]

As has already been stated, the paradox of salvation is rooted
in the paradox of the incarnation. This is the paradox that
God was in man and man was in God in the person of Jesus
Christ. This only can be considered "the Absolute Paradox."
All other paradoxes prove to be variations of this fundamental
one.[3] As Tillich rightly maintains, this paradox is not a logical
riddle but a new reality. It contradicts not the structure of
reason itself but rather the *doxa*, "the opinion which is based
on the whole of ordinary human experience including the empirical and the rational."[4] Whether Tillich perceives the full
dimensions of the paradox of the incarnation is another question.[5]

Human reason finds it difficult if not impossible to compre-
hend the paradoxes and mysteries of the workings of God.
This is not because these mysteries are irrational but because
natural reason is blind and arrogant. Calvin made this cogent
observation:

> All the mysteries of God are paradoxes to the flesh: and at
> the same time it possesses so much audacity, that it fears not to
> oppose them, and insolently to assail what it cannot compre-
> hend. We are hence reminded, that if we desire to become ca-
> pable of understanding them, we must especially labour to be-
> come free from our own reason, and to give up ourselves, and
> unreservedly to submit to his word.[6]

The paradox of salvation guards against the twin perils of
deterministic monergism and synergism. The first heresy makes

2 Westminster Confession, Ch. XVI, Art. III, in Philip Schaff, ed., *The
Creeds of Christendom*, Vol. III (New York: Harper & Brothers, 1919), pp.
633, 634.

3 See Paul Tillich, *Systematic Theology*, Vol. I (Chicago: University of
Chicago Press, 1951), p. 19; *Systematic Theology*, Vol. II (1957), p. 92;
Systematic Theology, Vol. III (1963), p. 57.

4 Paul Tillich, *Systematic Theology*, Vol. II, p. 92.

5 See explanatory note 29.

6 John Calvin, *Commentaries on the Epistle of Paul the Apostle to the
Romans*, trans. and ed. John Owen (Edinburgh: Calvin Translation Society,
1849), pp. 119, 120.

God alone the actor and reduces man to an automaton. The synergistic heresy affirms that man works alongside of God in the gaining of his salvation. The paradox asserts that it is not Christ in and of Himself but Christ in man who accomplishes our salvation; it is effectuated not by the independent or autonomous man who works with Christ but by the Spirit-empowered man, the man in Christ.

Whereas Roman Catholic theology is tempted to synergism, Reformed theology is constantly imperiled by monergism. By making God the sole cause and action in human salvation monergism fails to take seriously the decisive role of personal decision. A biblical theologian will certainly speak of God as the sole cause of salvation, but he will immediately add that faith is the sole means by which we lay hold of this salvation.

Adolf Köberle has made a bold and refreshing attempt to reappraise the soteriological paradox in his book *The Quest for Holiness*. He defines it as the paradox of God's sole activity in the working of salvation and of full human responsibility for its loss.[7] Yet this definition expresses only one side of the paradox. Man is also active in the working out of his salvation but only on the basis of divine grace. Also we must affirm that God withholds His salvation but only on the basis of man's sin. The paradox states that God is active in, with, and through man's activity. Therefore there is a sense in which God does all. Yet in another sense man is active too, from the beginning to the end, but only through the power of God's Spirit. The biblical understanding of the paradox excludes man's free will (*liberium arbitrium*) from the working of salvation, for otherwise this would place us again in the camp of synergism. It is to the credit of Köberle that he will have nothing to do with synergism of any kind.

The paradox of salvation has many facets and thereby lends itself to diverse formulations. Bonhoeffer expresses this paradox in terms of the inseparable connection of the gift of faith and the work of obedience: ". . . only he who believes is obe-

---

[7] Adolf Köberle, *The Quest for Holiness*, trans. John C. Mattes (Minneapolis: Augsburg Publishing House, 1938), pp. 142f., 228f.

dient, and only he who is obedient believes."[8] Bonhoeffer contends that if we stress only the first half of the proposition we end up with cheap grace. On the other hand, if we stress only the second part, then we have salvation by works, which is also a form of damnation.[9]

If we would relate the obedience of the Christian to the work of God in Christ on Calvary, then we can express the paradox in the following manner: "We can obey only through the power of the cross; the cross becomes efficacious only as we obey." It is important to retain the whole of this formulation not only in order to guard against the perils of cheap grace and works-righteousness but also to avoid the dangers of objectivism and subjectivism. Indeed, if we speak only of the first part of the proposition, then we end in objectivism; if we emphasize only the second part, then we are imperiled by a subjectivistic pattern of piety.

Contemporary theology has not always perceived the full importance of the paradox of salvation. Among those who have appeared to grasp the paradox (at least for the most part) are Bonhoeffer, Reinhold Niebuhr, Emil Brunner, Köberle, and Donald Baillie. Significantly, all of these men lean upon Kierkegaard to some degree. G. C. Berkouwer does not utilize the category of paradox as such, but he succeeds in retaining the essential correlation of justification and faith and also of faith and obedience. Such theologians as Aulén, Nygren, and Prenter have ended by rationalizing the paradox, although this was not their intention. Their heavy stress on justification by grace has prevented them from doing justice to the call to Christian perfection. J. K. S. Reid has sought to overcome the paradox in his book *Our Life in Christ*. He maintains that in Jesus Christ is to be found the perfect coincidence of divine and human freedom.[10] We contend, however, that this only points to the supreme paradox of the perfect unity of divine and

---

[8] Dietrich Bonhoeffer, *The Cost of Discipleship*, rev. and trans. R. H. Fuller (London: SCM Press, Ltd., 1959), p. 54.

[9] *Ibid.*, p. 58.

[10] See J. K. S. Reid, *Our Life in Christ* (Philadelphia: Westminster Press, 1963), p. 142.

human natures in the person of Jesus Christ. The paradox would seem to be heightened and underscored in his theology rather than overcome. Karl Barth speaks of two poles of salvation, but it is only the objective work of God in Christ that is regarded as decisively significant. For Barth salvation is primarily and essentially an "objective" event and only secondarily a "subjective" process. Bultmann and Ebeling have seen the interrelationship of faith and works, but they have lost sight of the objective historical basis of our salvation.

The Protestant Reformation recaptured the paradox of salvation but lost it again in its reaction against the Roman Catholic heresy of works-righteousness. Luther certainly perceives the paradox in his *Commentary on Romans*. But in the middle period of his theological development (particularly in his *Lectures on Galatians*) he often falls into the error of viewing justification as being almost wholly extrinsic to man. Calvin loses the paradox in his speculation on predestination and double-predestination. But theologians undercut the paradox of salvation by conceiving of faith as essentially passive. Although they always recognize the active dimension of faith, it is not given its proper emphasis in the framework of their theologies. In the famous dispute between Erasmus, who upheld the active side of faith, and Luther, who stressed the passive side, neither adequately grasped the paradox.[11]

The main streams of theology after the Reformation have generally failed to do justice to the paradox of salvation (although there are some noted individual exceptions). Although the Reformed doctrine of eternal security at first proved a powerful inspiration for action, eventually it prepared the way for complacency. Lutheran orthodoxy certainly succumbed to cheap grace by making baptism and assent to the faith guarantees of salvation. For the most part, orthodoxy has been tempted by cheap grace and objectivism. Liberalism and the liberal strand in Pietism have almost invariably ended up in works-righteousness and subjectivism. In Protestant orthodoxy the teachings and confessions of the church have been regarded as the ground of authority and assurance. In liberalism religious experience

11 See explanatory note 30.

has been the key to certainty. Neo-orthodoxy has tended to make the promises of Christ the basis for the assurance of salvation.

Our position is that Christian assurance is undercut if grounded in only one of the poles of authority, whether this be the experience and obedience of faithful man, the historical revelation of Christ as witnessed to in the Bible, the inward illumination of the Spirit, or the voice of the church. That is to say, we can trust the promises of Christ as revealed in Scripture only as we believe and obey (Heb. 4:1, 2). We can find security in the assurances given to us by the church only if we continually submit ourselves to Jesus Christ, the living Word of God. The apostle speaks of three witnesses — Spirit, water, and blood — and holds that these three agree (I Jn. 5:8). Our assurance is grounded not in the inward Spirit alone, for this would lead to spiritualism. But neither is our assurance to be located in the water or blood alone, for this would prepare the way for some kind of historical or sacramental objectivism. The ground of our assurance is the sacrifice of Christ on the cross, but it is always this sacrifice as apprehended by the eyes of faith (or in the inward light of the Spirit).

The early Luther warned against both a dependence on faith apart from Christ and a dependence on Christ apart from faith:

> Very instructively the apostle connects these two: "through Christ" and "through faith." . . . The first is directed against the presumptuousness of those who believe that they can have access to God without Christ, as if it were sufficient for them to have believed. So they want to come to God by faith alone, not through Christ but past Christ, as if they no longer needed Christ after having received the grace of justification. Secondly, he [Paul] turns against those who rely on too great a sense of security because of Christ and not because of faith, as if they could be saved through Christ without doing anything and without having to give any evidence of faith. They have too great a faith, nay, rather none at all. For both must be in effect: "through faith" and "through Christ," so that we do and endeavor everything possible in faith in Christ.[12]

---

[12] Martin Luther, *Luther: Lectures on Romans,* trans. and ed. Wilhelm Pauck (Philadelphia: Westminster Press, 1961), pp. 154, 155.

The paradox of salvation can be further illuminated by some critical questions. First of all, does the Christian life contribute to our final salvation? Seen as the work of the Holy Spirit, it does so contribute. But seen as the after-effect of this work in the sense of being our own work, it does not contribute. The Christian life is a fruit of the salvation (justification) already procured for us by Christ and a sign of our final salvation. It therefore can be considered a contributing element to our final salvation, since the fruit cannot be separated from the root. This holds true even in the case of the thief on the cross. To be sure, he did not have time to live a full Christian life. Yet the Christian life was implanted within him at the moment of his decision, since this life is none other than Christ living within us. To affirm that we cannot be saved apart from a Christian life consequently means that we cannot be saved unless Christ dwells within us.

At the same time we must hold that the Christian life cannot force God to grant us the gift of final salvation. We can in no wise merit nor earn our salvation. Faith brings us to the holy city, but only free grace opens the gate. And it is free grace alone that draws us in. What we receive is above anything that we deserve. The crown of righteousness is an *extra,* something beyond what we will or desire or merit.[13] The Christ within prepares us for coming glory, but He does not perfect us in this life. The Christian life is indispensable for salvation because the obedience of faith and a loving heart are necessary for the appropriation of the benefits of Christ's sacrifice. But the Christian life cannot merit salvation because our faith and love are inadequate.

At the same time we must contend that our works are necessary for receiving the gift of eternal life. They cannot obtain the right to final salvation, but they enable us to appropriate

---

13 Our position here is to be contrasted with that of Canon Cuttaz who writes: "It is a 'crown of justice' because it was promised and because it is due to merit. When the supreme Arbiter gives it, He accomplishes a work of equity. He does not award it as He pleases, according to His good pleasure or His preferences, but according to what is due . . . to those who have won it." Canon F. Cuttaz, *Our Life of Grace,* trans. Angeline Bouchard (Chicago: Fides Publishers Association, 1958) , p. 240.

this salvation. They prepare us to enjoy and lay hold of the treasures which are reserved for the faithful and obedient.

To determine the role of the Christian life in the plan of salvation we must inquire whether the Christian in and of himself contributes to his own salvation. We certainly do not make any positive contribution, for we have nothing to offer from our side that is acceptable in the light of divine justice. But our *faith* (which comes from God) contributes to our salvation. We can subscribe to the words of the hymn "Rock of Ages," written by an English Calvinist: "Nothing in my hand I bring,/Simply to thy cross I cling." But clinging simply and solely to the cross *is* the Christian life. We can therefore affirm that the Christian life contributes to our salvation because it strengthens our faith, not because it accumulates merit or wins satisfaction for us.

Even Calvin, who upheld the all-sufficiency of the sacrifice on the cross, nevertheless could speak of our sufferings and sacrifices as playing a role in our salvation:

> How much can it do to soften all the bitterness of the cross, that the more we are afflicted with adversities, the more surely our fellowship with Christ is confirmed! By communion with him the very sufferings themselves not only become blessed to us but also help much in promoting our salvation.[14]

Calvin here echoes Paul's contention that godly sorrow "produces a repentance that leads to salvation" (II Cor. 7:10). Neither Paul nor Calvin would wish to imply that our sufferings can actually gain us an entry into the kingdom. Rather, they mean that the suffering of faith makes us ready and willing to surrender to the Spirit of God, who alone can bring us salvation.

A second question to be asked which might throw further light on the soteriological paradox is whether the Christian can ever fall from grace. If this were possible, our salvation would certainly be contingent on our obedience. The Westminster Confession states that a man once justified "can never fall from

---

14 John Calvin, *Institutes*, III, 8, 1, p. 702.

the state of justification."[15] Pietists such as Spener held that we can lose our regeneration and that consequently we must be regenerated anew.

Our position is that we can fall from grace but only by not believing, by renouncing Christ. To be sure, we are all faithless in the sense that we do not obey God's law fully, but we are told that Christ is nevertheless faithful (II Tim. 2:13). Every Christian falls from grace by disobedience to God's law. Yet only through unbelief does one fall *out* of grace. It is not that we need a new regeneration but that we must return ever again to our baptism, the wellspring of regeneration. What is required is not a new work of grace; rather, we need to recover the grace that has been procured for us once for all by the sacrifice of Christ. Here again one can perceive the dialectical relation between grace and the obedience of faith. We cannot fall from grace so long as we believe; but the outside possibility is always there that we might some day cease to believe. Grace can be deemed irresistible only where faith is present.

Finally we must proffer the question whether we come to Christ by means of a free decision. We must reply in the affirmative, but at the same time it must be pointed out that this freedom is not our own but the free gift of God. It is given in the situation of hearing and preaching. To be retained this freedom must be returned to God (Kierkegaard). At the same time even this is not our own work but the work of God. The indispensable element in our salvation is not our holiness or good works but the decision of faith. Holiness and works of love contribute to our salvation insofar as they strengthen faith. But faith, that is, trusting and waiting upon the word of God, is "the one thing needful." Such faith will be crowned with perfect holiness at the end of our pilgrimage.

The paradox is that in ourselves we contribute nothing; in Christ we contribute everything. Fénelon expressed it in this way:

> Grace accomplishes everything in man, but it accomplishes everything with him and through him. Thus it is with grace that

[15] Westminster Confession, Ch. XI, Art. V. In Schaff, ed., *Creeds of Christendom*, Vol. III, p. 627. Cf. Canons of the Synod of Dort, Section V, Art. VIII.

I must act, forbear, suffer, wait, resist, believe, hope and love following all its impressions. It will accomplish everything in me. I shall accomplish everything through it.[16]

Yet we must point out that this "everything" which is accomplished by even the man in Christ is not the "all" that is essential. Even that which we can do through the Spirit is only that which involves human activity. We must remember that grace accomplishes much *for* man apart from his actions and even his faith. We cannot dethrone the principalities and powers as Christ did by His vicarious death on the cross. Nor can we procure the crown of righteousness that Christ won through His resurrection from the grave. Indeed, we contribute nothing of our own to the cross except our sins; we can offer for the crown only an imperfect holiness which by itself cannot suffice. Yet apart from this holiness no crown will be given to us.

The paradox is that God's election takes place in and through our decision and obedience. We are most active when we are most passive and absolutely dependent upon His power and working. Paul expressed this truth when he said, "I can do all things in him who strengthens me" (Phil. 4:13). Loyola voiced the paradoxical mystery of salvation when he said that we should work as if everything depended on ourselves and pray as if everything depended on God. Karl Barth has also recognized the paradox: "Faith is altogether the work of God, and it is altogether the work of man. It is a complete enslavement, and it is a complete liberation."[17]

Christ alone is the vine, but we are the branches. We must bear fruit, for otherwise we are cast forth and burned (Mt. 7: 19; Jn. 15:5, 6). As Luther put it, "Whoever begins to believe but does not always increase and grow finally loses his grace."[18] We are not justified by our fruits, but we are known and strengthened by our fruits. We are brought into the domain

---

[16] Francois Fénelon, *Christian Perfection*, ed. Charles Whiston, trans. Mildred Stillman (New York: Harper & Brothers, 1947), p. 129.

[17] Karl Barth, *Church Dogmatics*, Vol. III, Part 3, eds. G. W. Bromiley and T. F. Torrance, trans. G. W. Bromiley and R. J. Ehrlich (Edinburgh: T. & T. Clark, 1961), p. 247.

[18] Quoted in Adolf Köberle, *The Quest for Holiness*, p. 238.

of the kingdom by our faith, but we are kept in this domain by our fruits.

The fruit of faith is intimately linked with the root of divine grace; therefore it does indirectly contribute to our final salvation. That is to say, alien righteousness and actual righteousness are organically related. Yet the latter plays no part in the remission of sins. Actual righteousness or the fruits of faith contribute only to our sanctification. In our sanctification we are co-workers with Christ (I Cor. 3:5-9; II Cor. 6:1), but our role is always that of servant, not that of an equal partner.[19] We are instruments of God, not co-redeemers or co-mediators. Indeed, our sanctification is accomplished not by ascetic striving but by daily surrender to the Spirit within. Our hope depends not on our will or exertion but rather on God's mercy (Rom. 9:16). We hold not to self-sanctification but to sanctification by faith.

The only fruit of grace that can be regarded as absolutely necessary for salvation is faith itself (cf. Rom. 1:16, 17; 3:25, 26; 10:9, 10; Phil. 3:9; Eph. 3:12). In cases where the life of a recently converted Christian is suddenly cut off, we find only the presence of faith, for such a person does not have time to grow into holiness. But the gift of holiness need not be earned by a long period of suffering in purgatory; rather, it is given immediately to the Christian either at the time of his death or in the very brief transition from death into Paradise.[20]

Christ alone (*solus Christus*) accomplishes our salvation. But when we say this we must have in mind not only Christ on the cross but the mystical Christ, who meets us in daily experience. Christ must not be separated from the indwelling Holy Spirit. Nor can He be isolated from the faith and obedience of His disciples. The locus of salvation is not only the historical sacrifice of Christ but also the mystical presence of Christ in the sacramental community of the faithful.

---

[19] See explanatory note 31.

[20] This indeed is the view of Wesley who contending that perfect holiness is given only on the basis of faith and almost always at the time of death yet sometimes allowed for the fact that even after death more promises must be fulfilled in certain souls before they are finally taken into the presence of God. Harold Linstrom, *Wesley and Sanctification* (London: Epworth Press, n.d.), p. 204.

We also affirm that justification is by faith alone (*sola fide*).
But this is a faith that does not stand alone but which bears
fruit. It is a faith that works through love (Gal. 5:6).[21] Faith
is not only belief or intellectual assent; rather, it signifies wholehearted trust and commitment. It is a faith that is grounded
in the work of Christ and fulfilled in loving obedience. This
is why the apostle James asserts that we are justified by the faith
that gives rise to works and not by the faith that remains alone.[22]

Again, we affirm that we are justified by grace alone (*sola
gratia*). But this is a grace that realizes itself in faithful works.
Our good works are not the cause of the increase of faith but
rather the fruit of this increase. At the same time our works
are not simply a by-product of grace but the working out and
fruition of grace. Bonhoeffer has written: "The only man who
has the right to say that he is justified by grace alone is the
man who has left all to follow Christ."[23] This means that there
is no grace apart from Christian life. Yet since Christian life
is nothing other than Christ living in us, the glory must be given
not to the Christian but to Christ.

The perils today are works-righteousness and cheap grace.
Works-righteousness can be equated with moralism and legalism;
cheap grace can be associated with antinomianism. Both of these
patterns of deviation are to be seen as two sides of the same
coin, which might be labeled "easy salvation." At first glance
this category would seem not to apply to legalistic religion. Yet
if one is capable of procuring his salvation by doing certain
works, salvation becomes not very difficult after all. If salvation is located completely outside ourselves, either in a secret
divine decree or in the historical atonement or in baptism or
in the church, then grace becomes cheap. That is to say, grace
is assured to us without our having to give of ourselves, indeed
our very lives, for His service. On the other hand, if we locate
salvation in what we do, in our good works, or our decisions,
or our piety, then we have works-righteousness.

One of the more subtle kinds of works-righteousness is what

21 See explanatory note 32.
22 See explanatory note 33.
23 Dietrich Bonhoeffer, *The Cost of Discipleship*, p. 43.

has come to be known as faith-moralism. Here justification is attributed to faith, but faith is understood as primarily a work of man. It is no longer interpreted as a work of the Spirit within man enabling him to believe; rather, it is viewed as a result of man's conscious effort to arrive at the truth (with the aid of grace). Faith-moralism can be found in some strands of Protestant orthodoxy, particularly those in which faith is equated with assent to propositional truths. In this case we are not really justified by faith but rather by belief. Indeed, it can be said that in orthodoxy the righteousness of belief supplanted the righteousness of works as found in Roman Catholicism.

Faith-moralism can also be found in liberal Protestantism. In liberal theology we are justified not so much by our confession of faith as by our inner attitudes and feelings. It would be a caricature of liberalism to affirm that it holds to the view that what matters is not what we believe but whether we are sincere in our beliefs. Yet there is enough truth in this caricature to question whether the Reformation doctrine of *sola fide* has ever been grasped in liberal theology. Ménégoz maintains that the hallmark of Protestant liberalism is that one is justified by faith independently of belief.[24] Popular culture religion in this country is definitely permeated by faith-moralism. It is not faith in a living God but faith in faith that characterizes American folk or cultural religion.[25]

Yet it would not be wise to minimize the role of faith in our salvation. In our judgment both Torrance and Tillich fail to do justice to the biblical truth that faith is the means by which we are justified.[26] It is true that we are justified *through* faith by grace, but it is also true that we are justified *by* faith. Certainly this was the viewpoint of St. Paul (cf. Rom. 5:1; Gal. 2:

24 See Louis Bouyer, *The Spirit and Forms of Protestantism*, p. 59.

25 For a penetrating study of American cultural religion see Martin E. Marty, *The New Shape of American Religion* (New York: Harper & Bros., 1958). Also see Louis Schneider and Sanford M. Dornbusch, *Popular Religion* (Chicago: University of Chicago Press, 1958).

26 For Tillich's criticism of *sola fide* see Paul Tillich, *Systematic Theology*, Vol. III, p. 224. Torrance prefers the expression "justification by Christ alone" to *sola fide*. See his article "Justification" in *Christianity Divided*, eds. Daniel J. Callahan, et al. (New York: Sheed & Ward, 1961), pp. 293, 294.

16). *Sola fide* is certainly a basic truth in Scripture, but it lends itself to profound misinterpretation from various sides. This truth is endangered when it is isolated from other Scriptural truths such as the call to sainthood or holiness.

We need today to recapture the paradox of salvation. In doing this we will at the same time recapture the significance of the Christian life. Anyone can affirm a paradox. But to hold onto the paradox in working out one's faith is a very difficult task. If we avoid the paradox, then we blur the scandal of the cross and have not a simple gospel but a simplified one. We then have not the whole gospel but a fragmented and distorted one.

It is imperative that we discern again that the kingdom is both a gift and a task. The cross must not only be received but also carried. The light of the gospel must not only be believed in but also lifted up before the world. The elect are those who persevere to the end. The saved are those who strive to work out their salvation in fear and trembling. It is indeed a fearful thing to undertake the task of "becoming a Christian" (Kierkegaard). *he viewed from human effort, but we must look from God's grace in which there is no fear!*

To hold onto the paradox is primarily a matter not of understanding but of confession and obedience. To affirm the paradox means the abdication of the understanding so that faith might live. But this does not entail the abandoning of reason. Indeed, a zeal without knowledge is blind (Rom. 10:2). We must use our reason to show that faith transcends the understanding. Reason must be made the servant of faith. We should bow before the mystery of faith. The norm for truth must be viewed as faithful reasoning or fidelity, not clarity. We must strive to think as mature Christians, but we are called to trust and believe as little children.

Explanatory Notes

Introduction

1. The secular or radical theologians have drastically reinterpreted soteriology. They view reconciliation in terms of the breaking down of the social barriers that divide men — and one must acknowledge that it does have a social or horizontal dimension — but at the same time they fail to connect this social reconciliation with the reconciling work of God in Jesus Christ. Nor do they adequately relate it to the converting work of the Holy Spirit apart from which there can be no reconciliation of classes or races. There is a tendency among the secular theologians to conceive of the arena of salvation as the present struggle for social and racial equality. We, on the contrary, equate it with the daily crisis of repentance and faith, a crisis that must not be separated from, but rather arises out of the crisis of the death and resurrection of Jesus Christ by which the foundations of our salvation were laid. A life of penitence and faith may very well entail participation in the battle against injustice and corruption in society. Yet this warfare will be waged with different motivations from those of the man of the world, and it will be directed towards ultimately different ends.

2. Traditional Roman Catholic theology conceives of God as the primary cause in human salvation and man's cooperation as the secondary cause. Our position is that God is the sole cause of human salvation, but that He works in and through man. Our salvation is to be attributed to God alone, but He completes His saving work by means of man's faith and obedience. We could regard faith as an instrumental cause of salvation provided that this does not mean that man is an automaton and that his personal response is of no decisive significance. Even in the process of being liberated from enslavement to sin he is not an automaton because he actively resists God's grace even while seeking for help from beyond himself. Once having been freed from the rule of sin he must now make an active decision to accept his new freedom, but the paradox is that he can choose to remain with Christ only insofar as he is moved and empowered by the Spirit to do so. We must guard against both the view that man can

141

contribute to his salvation on the basis of his own strength or free will and the view that salvation is effected apart from man's faith and obedience.

3. Mention might also be made of the Anabaptists, who anticipated many of the emphases of the Pietists and the later evangelicals. Unlike these later movements the Anabaptists developed in opposition to rather than out of the main stream of the Protestant Reformation. Much of their orientation is pre-Reformation; yet their concern for the new birth and a life of discipleship gives them a certain affinity with Pietism and Evangelicalism. See George Williams, *The Radical Reformation* (Philadelphia: Westminster Press, 1962).

Chapter 1: The Plan of Salvation

4. Karl Barth, *Church Dogmatics*, eds. G. W. Bromiley and T. F. Torrance, trans. G. W. Bromiley (Edinburgh: T. & T. Clark, 1956), IV, 1, p. 775. Barth tends to modify his emphasis on the objectivity of redemption in a later volume of his *Church Dogmatics*, where he acknowledges that the decision of faith can be regarded in a secondary or limited sense as an "event of salvation" (IV, 3, a, p. 220). Yet his general position even in his later writings is that faith is (in Gollwitzer's words) "subsequential and non-fundamental." For a defense of Barth at this point against the criticisms of Ebeling see Helmut Gollwitzer, *The Existence of God as Confessed by Faith*, trans. James Leitch (Philadelphia: Westminster Press, 1965), pp. 138, 139.

We hold that salvation has its objective basis in the saving work on Calvary but is realized in our lives only in the decision of faith. The gates of the prison in which we find ourselves have been opened by the objective work of Christ, but we cannot be said to be "saved" until we are moved and empowered to walk through these gates to freedom. Only when we enter the fullness of Christian freedom can we then speak of the work of Christ on the cross as the objective reality of our salvation.

5. We here have in mind Calvin's distinction between *fides* and *fiducia*. Calvin maintained that *fiducia* (trust) is the consequence of *fides* (the inner or personal knowledge of Christ's salvation). By *fides* Calvin did not mean a mere historical knowledge of the gospel but rather a spiritual apprehension of Christ implanted within man by the Holy Spirit. See Walter E. Stuermann, *A Critical Study of Calvin's Concept of Faith* (Ann Arbor, Michigan: Edwards Brothers, Inc., 1952), pp. 46-48, 102, 106. Since this spiritual apprehension involves not only the illumination of the mind but also the conversion of the heart, it certainly can be included in what many Lutheran and Reformed scholars have called *fiducia cordis* (the sincere confidence of the heart in the gospel). At the same time Calvin sought to safe-

guard the divine initiative in our salvation and therefore made personal trust and confidence contingent upon the spiritual knowledge imparted to man by the Spirit of God.

Chapter 2: The Various Meanings of Salvation

6. See Hans Küng, "Justification and Sanctification According to the New Testament," in Daniel J. Callahan, Heiko A. Oberman, and Daniel J. O'Hanlon, *Christianity Divided* (New York: Sheed & Ward, 1961), pp. 308-335. Küng rightly points out that God's justification and God's sanctification are two sides of the one act of salvation, but that God's justification and man's sanctification are two steps in the process of salvation with the latter being based on the former (see p. 331). In traditional Catholic theology justification is absorbed into sanctification. Küng is to be given credit for distinguishing these two sides or dimensions of salvation. For a fuller statement of Küng's views on this subject see his work *Justification,* trans. Thomas Collins, Edmund Tolk, and David Granskow (New York: Thomas Nelson & Sons, 1964). In his introduction Karl Barth raises the question whether Küng correctly interprets the teaching of the Roman Catholic Church on justification.

7. Wesley maintained that "entire sanctification," which he also called "perfect love" and "sinless perfection" (a term he finally abandoned), could be given to Christians in this life in the sense that they could be made free from voluntary transgressions or sins. We hold that perfect love (*agape*) can be experienced and exercised by the Christian in this life, but that it can be exercised only in an imperfect way. Now we have a "foretaste" of perfect love, but we are not perfected in love until our sinful desire has been entirely extirpated. It must be recognized that Wesley distinguished between a relative perfection which is basically a perfection in intention and an absolute perfection in which even our weaknesses and infirmities are overcome. He held that this latter perfection is not possible in this life. For a fuller statement of Wesley's position on Christian perfection see Philip Watson, ed., *The Message of the Wesleys* (New York: Macmillan Co., 1964), pp. 195-220; and Harold Linstrom, *Wesley and Sanctification* (London: Epworth Press, n.d), pp. 105-160.

One reason why Wesley could speak of the possibility of a perfection in love or a sinless perfection in this life is that he defined sin as a voluntary transgression of a known law of God and thereby did not fully acknowledge the penetration of sin into the unconscious life of man. Nor did he give sufficient attention to the collective dimensions of sin.

8. Among those who have endeavored to relate the theological meanings of salvation to the insights of contemporary psychiatry is James G. Emerson. Emerson, writing as a pastoral psychologist, main-

tains that there is a discernible correlation between the realization of forgiveness and the integrated life as viewed by psychiatry. One problem is that integration between one's actions and one's conscience (which is the theological understanding of wholeness) does not always coincide with the integration of one's values and the values of the culture (which is very often the criterion of wholeness in secular psychiatry). See James G. Emerson, Jr., *The Dynamics of Forgiveness* (Philadelphia: Westminster Press, 1964).

A recent attempt by a Christian psychiatrist to relate theology and psychiatry is T. Bovet's *The Road to Salvation,* trans. F. A. Baker (Garden City, New York: Doubleday and Co., 1964). Bovet writes basically from the perspective of Christian faith and for the most part successfully resists the temptation to subordinate theological to philosophical categories. As in so many other books of this nature the emphasis is on the present experience of salvation, and the eschatological dimension of salvation is minimized (although not denied).

9. Martin Luther, *Luther: Lectures on Romans,* ed. and trans. Wilhelm Pauck (Philadelphia: Westminster Press, 1961), p. 112. In this commentary Luther tends to include sanctification within justification. In the middle period of his development (represented by his second *Commentary on Galatians* [1535] and *The Bondage of the Will*) he upholds extrinsic justification although he generally seeks to relate this to sanctification or personal holiness. Yet even in his *Commentary on Galatians* he could write: "We have indeed begun to be justified by faith, by which we have also received the first fruits of the Spirit; and the mortification of our flesh has begun. But we are not yet perfectly righteous. Our being justified perfectly still remains to be seen, and this is what we hope for." *Luther's Works,* Vol. 27, ed. and trans. Jaroslav Pelikan (St. Louis: Concordia, 1964), p. 21.

10. Our position on the goal of salvation diverges from that of Bonhoeffer in his *Letters and Papers from Prison.* He understands this goal or hope solely in terms of a new life in this world. He contends that biblical faith "speaks of *historical* redemption, i.e., redemption on this side of death, whereas the myths of salvation are concerned to offer men deliverance from death. . . . The difference between the Christian hope of resurrection and a mythological hope is that the Christian hope sends a man back to his life on earth in a wholly new way. . . ." Dietrich Bonhoeffer, *Letters and Papers from Prison,* ed. Eberhard Bethge, trans. Reginald Fuller (New York: Macmillan Co., 1953), p. 205. The truth in Bonhoeffer's allegation is that the Christian hope does relate to life in this world, but he fails to perceive that this hope is directed to life in eternity. We hold that Reinhold Niebuhr is a better guide at this point in that he affirms that the kingdom of God is "beyond history" and that every realization of God's salvation in this life can only be partial and fragmentary.

Chapter 3: The Divine Sacrifice

11. For Wieman the Christian revelation consists in creative good overpowering Jesus and also the company of the first disciples and continuing to exert a redemptive influence wherever men cease to cling to created good and open themselves to the source of human good. The death of Jesus was not a vicarious sacrifice for sin but the occasion for the release of the creative event in history. It was not Jesus who rose from the dead but rather "life-transforming creativity" or "creative power." To the credit of Wieman, he seems to emphasize the objective and historical character of the events of salvation in a way that Bultmann fails to do. But by separating Christ from Jesus, he fails to do justice to the uniqueness of the person of Jesus Christ and the decisive significance of His sacrifice on the cross. See his *The Source of Human Good* (Chicago: University of Chicago Press, 1946).

Ogden, who seeks to incorporate existentialist insights into a process philosophy, maintains in his book *Christ Without Myth* (New York: Harper & Row, 1961) that there is no saving work performed by Christ: Jesus Christ is simply a decisive manifestation of that primal healing love which makes authentic life possible (pp. 132f., 142f.). Salvation consists essentially in the realization of authentic existence which is a universal or ever-present possibility.

12. Karl Barth, *Church Dogmatics*, IV, 1, ed. G. W. Bromiley and T. F. Torrance, trans. G. W. Bromiley (Edinburgh: T. & T. Clark, 1956), p. 643. Certainly in one sense Jesus Christ can be referred to as the subjective pole of the atonement in that He is the Representative of fallen humanity. But Jesus Christ is nevertheless objective to us, and there still remains the necessity for the realization of salvation in our own lives. Inasmuch as Christ becomes the "new man" within us through baptism and faith, He can be spoken of as the subjective side of redemption in another sense. But Barth does not give sufficient recognition to this second and equally crucial aspect of Christ's activity, which is correlative with the Christian life. Barth makes a place for the appropriation of Christ's salvation in his doctrine of the Holy Spirit, but he refrains from speaking of a "mystical union" with Christ.

Chapter 4: Bearing the Cross

13. Bultmann rightly points out in his analysis of the word "faith" (*pistis*) in Kittel's *Theologisches Wörterbuch zum Neuen Testament* (Vol. IV) that faith in the New Testament has various meanings, including obedience, acceptance, trust, faithfulness, and Christian doctrine (*fides quae creditur*). For the translation see Rudolf Bultmann and Arthur Weiser, *Faith*, trans. Dorothea Barton (London: Adam & Charles Black, 1961). Bultmann maintains that the basic

meaning of *pistis* is obedient acceptance of the kerygma. We maintain that although faith and obedience are often inseparable in the New Testament, there are dimensions of faith that cannot be subsumed under the category of obedience. Bultmann tends to ignore that aspect of faith which some theologians have designated as *notitia spiritualis* (cf. John T. Mueller). This signifies the inward spiritual conviction or experiential knowledge that comes to man by virtue of being grasped by the Spirit of God. Certainly the definition of faith as given in Hebrews 11:1 is not equivalent to obedience or acceptance (cf. Philem. 6; Col. 2:7; I Thes. 3:2; I Tim. 1:5). Ephesians 2:8, 9 would seem to exclude the role of obedience in faith, although what is actually excluded is what man can do through his own power. There are several passages in the New Testament that conjoin that aspect of faith which is *believing* (or accepting) and that aspect which is *knowing,* and in which the former is made to depend upon the latter (cf. Jn. 16:30; 17:8; I Jn. 4:16). Of course, faith in the sense of believing is the basis for the fulfillment of our knowledge of Christ. We also must affirm that knowledge (*gnosis*) must be included in faith (*pistis*), or else it is not true knowledge but only opinion.

In forming a systematic doctrine of faith, we must not simply take as our norm the literal meanings of *pistis* and its derivatives. Rather, we should seek to ascertain how these meanings are related to the total picture in the New Testament (and indeed in the entire Bible) of how man comes to a saving knowledge of God. Certainly it is a basic contention of the New Testament that before one can turn to God and believe, one's eyes must be opened by the Spirit of God (cf. Acts 26:18; Jn. 3:5; 12:36).

14. In line with the fathers of the Reformed Church we hold that our acceptance (*assensus*) is not simply intellectual assent to the gospel but heartfelt or practical assent, i.e., the acceptance of the whole man. Similarly the knowledge of faith (*notitia*) is not merely theoretical but existential and experiential. Many of the Reformed (and also Lutheran) fathers held that *assensus* and *notitia* are included in *fiducia* (meaning trust or reliance), since the will is involved in both our assent and our knowledge. That is, our assent is a trusting assent and our knowledge is a trusting and confident knowledge. Yet *fides* cannot simply be reduced to *fiducia*, since this term does not adequately cover the cognitive and ethical dimensions of faith. If we were to select an English term that would retain the various nuances of *fiducia* as well as of *assensus* and *notitia* it would be the term "commitment." Commitment entails knowledge, assent, and trust as well as obedience.

15. All suffering is made possible by sin, although no particular affliction is to be attributed necessarily to a specific sin. At the same time every kind of suffering can be made to serve the good of others and the advancement of the kingdom. To offer up one's affliction

to God means that one is seeking to let the Holy Spirit use one's affliction for God's glory. Someone who is blind, for example, might be led by the Spirit to find in his affliction the means by which he is enabled to draw near to God in meditation and prayer. In drawing close to God he is also drawn closer to his fellow man as he is awakened to their needs and moved to make intercession for them. Again, a blind person might learn Braille and bring cheer to others by personal correspondence or by translating or writing works of edification for afflicted brethren (as did Helen Keller). He might also teach the outside world what it means to live only by the light of faith. Still again, he might pray to be healed of his infirmity so that the new eon might become manifest to the world and also so that he might be free to serve God in a new way. Some theologians (in Roman and high Anglican circles) suggest that he might also pray that his affliction be made a channel or means by which others are converted or by which the suffering of others is mitigated. This idea must be treated with caution, since our suffering cannot atone for the sins of others. But in God's providence certainly our afflictions might be used to point others to the one who does remit sin. And might they not also be instrumental in alleviating the temporal consequences of the sins of others if in our intercessions we pray that we might suffer in place of or with another?

16. Luther's life and ministry are reminders to all Christians that loyalty to the Word of God takes priority not only over the biological family but also over the ecclesiastical family. They also witness to the fact that the cares of monastic or community life and the pretensions to righteousness that such a life may entail can choke our fellowship with Christ as much as the cares and attachments of the natural family.

17. Courvoisier reminds us that Zwingli died as a chaplain in the Protestant army. But he actively entered the battle when he saw that his side was being overwhelmed. "Information concerning his death is to be found in the writings of Myconius, Bucer, and Bullinger. They state that Zwingli, seeing some of his people overwhelmed by a great number of enemies, threw himself actively into the battle to either save them or die with them. Hit several times, he fell and, in the evening after the battle, was found by the victorious soldiers. Lying on the ground, dying, unable to speak, hands joined as for prayer, eyes raised to heaven. Identified as a 'heretic' he was reviled and finally killed by a captain from Unterwald. His body was then burned and his ashes scattered." Jacques Courvoisier, *Zwingli: A Reformed Theologian* (Richmond: John Knox Press, 1963), p. 25.

18. To be sure, in Catholic theology salvation can be earned only with the aid of grace, but the emphasis has often been (particularly in popular Catholicism) much more on the earning than on the

grace. A recent German Catholic catechism says: "Every good work that we do while we are in the state of grace earns for us an increase of grace here on earth and an everlasting reward in heaven. . . . We must do our utmost to avoid sin, and by means of good works earn merits for heaven." *A Catholic Catechism* (New York: Herder & Herder, 1957), pp. 199, 200, 369.

19. This position is held by Karl Barth as well as by many others who stand very close to him on the doctrine of salvation. To be sure, Barth contends that although *man* can only acknowledge and witness to his salvation, *God* can and does effect a change within man that accompanies man's response. Faith itself is only cognitive, but through faith the benefits of salvation are implanted within man. Faith is basically a human action, but "in this action there begins and takes place a new and particular being of man." *Church Dogmatics,* ed. G. W. Bromiley and T. F. Torrance, trans. G. W. Bromiley (Edinburgh: T. & T. Clark, 1956), p. 749. Yet in Barth's thinking salvation takes place not in man but in Christ who represents man. What takes place in man is the effect of salvation (although this too can be regarded as "salvation" in a secondary sense).

Chapter 5: The Crown of Glory

20. The question concerning final certainty of our salvation (*certitudo salutis*) has occupied the attention of theologians through the ages. The Roman Catholic position is that we cannot have such certainty in this life and consequently there is always need for additional meritorious works. Against the Roman view Luther held that we can have certainty of salvation through faith in Jesus Christ. Classical Calvinism taught that certainty is a possible but not necessary fruit of salvation. Our regeneration depends on our election, but a sure knowledge of our election does not necessarily follow. Evangelicalism stressed the subjective consciousness of assurance as being vital to our salvation. Our position is that assurance is not something static but something dynamic. It is conditional upon our relationship with Christ. We can know we are saved when we look to the promises of Christ and not to our own feelings or experiences. We can have assurance when we cease struggling to gain assurance as a tangible psychic reality and seek to lay hold of the mercy of Christ. The paradox is that we can have security when we renounce our own security and cast ourselves on the security of Christ.

Our view approaches that of the German Dominican Stephen Pfürtner in his *Luther and Aquinas on Salvation,* trans. Edward Quinn (New York: Sheed & Ward, 1964). Pfürtner, in seeking to give a faithful restatement of Aquinas' position, maintains that the Christian, although lacking final certainty of being in a state of grace, nevertheless does have a certain hope and confidence in Christ's mercy. We hold that the Christian can be sure that he is in a state of grace so long as he looks to Christ for his salvation.

21. It must be recognized that for Wesley "Christian perfection," "perfect love," and "entire sanctification" are not synonymous with glorification. In Wesley's mind Christian perfection can be attained in this life and therefore precedes glorification. We contend that the term "Christian perfection" should be reserved for perfection in its fullness, or final perfection. Just as we already partake of the glory that is to be revealed, so we now have a foretaste of our future perfection. But this perfection is always a goal and never a possession. The Christian can attain a certain measure of spiritual maturity in this life, but perfection in its fullness is not yet within his grasp. Jesus did possess perfect love in its fullness in this life, but He is also pictured as being in an incipient state of glory although His glory was generally hidden, and only on occasions did it become visible (cf. Lk. 9:32; Jn. 1:14). It is interesting to note that Wesley himself never claimed to have reached Christian perfection.

22. When Jesus called His disciples to be perfect as God is perfect (Mt. 5:48) He was confronting them with what Reinhold Niebuhr aptly calls "an impossible possibility." Niebuhr holds (against Christian orthodoxy) that the ideal of perfect love can be realized through God's grace, and this is why Jesus' command is forever relevant. At the same time Niebuhr insists (against all forms of utopianism) that every realization of this ideal in human history proves to be only an approximation of the ideal. This is why we must say that the kingdom is always coming but that it is never here. For Niebuhr's views on the relevance of an "impossible ethical ideal" see his *An Interpretation of Christian Ethics* (New York: Harper & Bros., 1935), pp. 35-62, 101-136. However, Niebuhr does not take into sufficient consideration the fact that the ideal was perfectly realized in Jesus. Niebuhr more explicitly affirms the incarnation of perfect love in Jesus in subsequent works, but by denying the sinlessness of Jesus and speaking of the triumph over sin occurring at the "edge of history," he does not succeed in doing justice to the biblical paradox that Jesus is both God and man. Niebuhr is correct in his judgment that sinful man can only realize the ideal of love imperfectly and fragmentarily. He is also sound in his view that the call to perfection is not only a divine command addressed to man but also a divine judgment upon man.

23. Thomas Aquinas rejected the view that a fallen man could merit the grace of conversion even *de congruo*. But many Catholic theologians subsequently have held the contrary. Pohle writes: ". . . we hold that even a man in mortal sin, provided he co-operate with the first grace of conversion, is able to merit *de congruo* by his supernatural acts not only a series of graces which will lead to conversion, but finally justification itself." See J. Pohle, "Merit" in *The*

Catholic Encyclopedia, ed. Charles Herbermann, *et al.* (New York: Gilmary Society, 1911). The whole idea of merit is now being carefully reappraised by Roman Catholic ecumenicists. For a pungent criticism of the theology of merit by a lay Roman Catholic see Ida F. Görres, *The Hidden Face,* trans. Richard and Clara Winston (New York: Pantheon Books, Inc., 1959). See also Hans Küng, *Justification,* trans. Thomas Collins, *et al.* (New York: Thomas Nelson, 1964), pp. 188f., 270-274.

24. Jesus does away with the idea of merit and reward in the strict sense by comparing the relation of God to men with that of a master and his household servants (cf. Mt. 24:45f.; 25:14f.; Lk.17:9). In Matthew 20:1f., where Jesus actually speaks of paid laborers and so leaves the door open for the strict idea of reward according to merit, He emphasizes by contrast the truth that God will not be bound by this rule but reserves to Himself the right of graciously transcending it.

25. Bishop Sheen has written: "The Church is a spiritual banker. It has all the merits of the Passion of Our Lord and the Blessed Mother, the merits of the martyrs, saints, and confessors, and the patient endurance of persecution in the present time: all of these merits are far greater than those needed for the salvation of these saintly and good people. The Church takes that surplus, puts it into her treasury, and bids all her weak and wounded, who cannot pay all the debts they owe for their sins, to draw on those reserves." Fulton J. Sheen, *These Are the Sacraments* (New York: Hawthorne Books, Inc., 1962), p. 87. Cf. The Baltimore Catechism: "The superabundant satisfaction of the Blessed Virgin Mary and of the saints is that which they gained during their lifetime but did not need, and which the Church applies to their fellow members of the communion of saints." *The New Revised Baltimore Catechism and Mass* (New York: Benziger Bros., 1949), p. 250.

26. "Sheol" referred originally to a shadowy subhuman world beyond the grave. In the later Old Testament and intertestamental periods Sheol signified the realm of departed spirits, with a distinction being made between the righteous and the unrighteous. Hades in the New Testament is roughly equivalent with the later meaning of Sheol. The predominant view in the New Testament is that Hades is the general abode of the dead, but the connotation is basically negative. In Luke 16:19-31 Hades is pictured as a place of punishment, although some commentators understand this parable as referring to two separate regions of Hades. In the book of Revelation Hades represents a place of anguish for the departed who do not know Christ. At the same time it is definitely distinguished from "the bottomless pit" where evil spirits dwell and "the lake of fire" where all the hosts of wickedness will finally be cast. Our term for this interim state of waiting and affliction is the "World of Spirits," which is roughly identi-

cal with the more limited meaning of Hades. This idea of an interim intermediate state for the wicked as well as for the righteous was present among many of the early church fathers.

Chapter 6: The Christian Pilgrimage

27. Niebuhr's thinking reflects one strand in Reformation piety, but he does not do justice to the other strand in the Reformation, which speaks of growth in personal holiness. He does make a place for "Christ in us" as well as "Christ for us," but he does not take into sufficient consideration that the man in Christ has experienced not only forgiveness but also an internal or ontological change. The Christian is a new person, although not yet perfected or fully restored. Niebuhr's emphasis is on the justification of God rather than the sanctification of man, and this accounts for his overt pessimism concerning the moral capabilities of the Christian. His relative optimism regarding the possibility of a limited form of human progress is derived from the Renaissance conception of the "infinite possibilities of man" and not from the regeneration of men in Christ effected by faith. Despite his affinity with the piety of the Reformation, Niebuhr goes beyond the Reformation at several crucial points (thereby reflecting his liberal and pietistic background). One of these points is his belief that the most potent form of Christian witness is a life of outgoing love.

28. Religious enthusiasm might be defined as a rapturous state of devotion born out of a crisis experience and based on the belief that one can be totally possessed by God in the here and now. The word literally means "in God" (*en theos*). According to Ronald Knox in his book *Enthusiasm* (Oxford: Clarendon Press, 1950), the hallmark of religious enthusiasm is the belief that nature is replaced by grace in the redeemed (p. 3). This is a type of perfectionism that denies the presence of any unwholesome desire or moral defection in the man of God. Moreover, it is held that the man under grace receives direct and immediate guidance from God and that this spiritual guidance takes precedence over the written word. The Holiness and Pentecostal sects are constantly imperiled by religious enthusiasm in that they speak of a continuous or permanent state of entire sanctification that can be obtained by the Christian in this life. This is the reason why many of these sects have no place for a prayer of confession in their worship services. Also for many of these groups the basis of authority is the present inspiration of the Spirit and not the biblical canon and creeds of the church. Wesley cannot be spoken of as an enthusiast because he acknowledged that the Christian is never totally free from transgressions (albeit involuntary transgressions) and that even the sanctified need to repent. Wesley also preferred to speak of the full Christian life as a "moment-by-moment" life as over

against a "state of entire sanctification." (See W. E. Sangster, *The Path to Perfection* [Nashville: Abingdon, 1943], pp. 109-112). Moreover, for Wesley no Christian is so perfect that he need no longer subject his experiences to the criterion of Holy Scripture.

Chapter 7: The Paradox of Salvation

29. Despite the brilliant insights of Tillich concerning Jesus Christ as the final or absolute paradox, he cannot bring himself to affirm the full truth of this paradox, namely, that God *became* man in Jesus Christ. Tillich is willing to assert that God manifested Himself in the person of Jesus, but not that God actually became (*egeneto*) a man. Consequently his Christology is deficient, since he fails to grasp the ontological unity between the humanity and deity of Jesus Christ. Therefore he speaks of "Jesus as the Christ" or the Christ who appeared in Jesus, but not Jesus Christ, the God-Man. See his *Systematic Theology*, Vol. II, pp. 149, 150.

Donald Baillie in his very scholarly and penetrating study *God Was In Christ* (New York: Charles Scribner's Sons, 1948) also fails to grasp the full import of the Christological paradox. He expresses this paradox in terms of the conjunction of divine grace and human freedom in the person of Jesus. This is surely one manifestation of the deeper paradox. But certainly the foundational paradox is an ontological one — the infinite and almighty God incarnating Himself in a finite and weak human vessel. This was the paradox that Kierkegaard perceived so incisively, but it is precisely this paradox which Baillie (and also Tillich) seemingly refuse to accept. It must also be said that Baillie does not do justice to what we have called the soteriological paradox. This is more than simply the conjunction of grace and human freedom. It signifies the coalescence of divine grace and a restored or divinely given freedom.

30. Louis Bouyer is probably right in his criticisms of both Luther and Erasmus in their classic debate on the bondage of the will. Bouyer writes: "For both Erasmus and Luther, to say that God and man act together in justification must mean that their joint action is analogous to that of two men drawing the same load. Consequently, the more one does, the less the other; whence, for Luther, realizing anew that grace does everything in salvation, it follows of necessity that man does nothing. But Erasmus desired to uphold the other aspect of tradition; that salvation is truly ours implies that we are ourselves active; it is far from covering us with a cloak that would leave us unchanged and merely passive. Hence the necessity that God does not do all, that his grace is simply an aid from outside, not the source of the saving action which must come from us." Louis Bouyer, *The Spirit and Forms of Protestantism*, trans. A. V. Littledale (Westminster, Maryland: Newman Press, 1956), pp. 156, 157.

31. Hans Küng follows Barth in speaking of man as a "covenant partner" of God. See his *Justification,* trans. Thomas Collins, Edmund E. Tolk, and David Granskow (New York: Thomas Nelson & Sons, 1964). Küng insists that man can in no wise cooperate in his conversion to partnership with God; he must be made a partner by divine grace. But once he has been given partnership he is then empowered to cooperate with God in the task of Christian mission. Küng describes this cooperation in terms of involvement in an activity which God alone has executed. "It is a cooperation *(Mitwirken)* not in the sense of collaboration *(Mitwerken)* but of involvement *(Mitmachen)*" (p. 264). Küng for the most part successfully eschews the synergism which has so often characterized Catholic theology, although he occasionally lapses into traditional Catholic thought patterns when, for example, he posits a universal capacity within man to respond to grace: "For this purpose He has, through His prevenient grace, preserved in the perishing sinner the power, the understanding, and the ability to choose" (p. 264). Küng's contention that his views reflect the mind of the Council of Trent is open to question, although he amasses an imposing array of evidence. Küng's work is to be welcomed as an outstanding contribution to the ecumenical dialogue.

32. We will not support, however, the medieval formulation of "faith formed by love" *(fides caritate formata)*. In Roman Catholic scholastic theology faith by itself is regarded as deficient for justification and therefore must be formed or perfected by love. In our position faith by itself justifies, but it is always accompanied by love. Faith needs to be strengthened and fulfilled in a life of service but only because the goal of justification is sanctification. Love also must be fulfilled and deepened, but it can only do so when it is undergirded and sustained by faith.

33. It is interesting to note that neither Calvin nor Luther did justice to the assertion of James that we are justified by works and not by faith alone (Jas. 2:24). Calvin in his *Commentary on James* significantly by-passes this verse. It was Calvin's view that Paul and James conceive of justification in different ways. Paul thinks of justification in the sight of God, whereas James thinks of justification in the sight of men. This is not very convincing. Luther resolved the problem by questioning the apostolic character of James. Wesley is much better here in that he contends that Paul and James are speaking about different kinds of faith as well as different kinds of works. According to Wesley Paul's idea of faith is wholehearted commitment and trust; James thinks of faith in terms of intellectual or outward assent. Paul is speaking of the works of the law, i.e., works antecedent to faith, whereas James has in mind the fruits of faith or works subsequent to faith. For a good discussion of Wesley's attempt to reconcile Paul and James see Arthur Crabtree, *The Restored Relationship* (Valley Forge, Pa.: Judson Press, 1963), pp. 152-155.

Index of Subjects

Index of Names

Index of Scripture

161